Houghton
Mifflin
Harcourt

PERFORMANCE ASSESSMENT

4

Welcome Students,

The more you practice something, the better you get at it. With *Performance Assessment*, you will have the chance to practice reading and writing

- ▶ **opinion essays**
- ▶ **informative essays**
- ▶ **literary analysis**
- ▶ **narratives**

In each unit, you will master one of these types of writing by following three simple steps.

- ▶ **Analyze the Model**
- ▶ **Practice the Task**
- ▶ **Perform the Task**

As you follow these steps, you'll find yourself building the confidence you need to succeed at performance assessments. Let's get started!

Unit 1 Opinion Essay
Eye on the Environment

Step 1 • Analyze the Model

Should people use disposable bags?

Read Source Materials

Magazine Editorial
"Reduce" is the New "Recycle" by Rita Amore 4

Letter to the Editor
from Anthony Murray... 6

Student Model
Is Just Recycling Enough? by Taniya Thomas 8

Step 2 • Practice the Task

Should dogs be allowed on the beach?

Read Source Materials

Letter to the Editor
from Amanda Evans.. 12

Petition
from Dog-Owners' Association of Monterey....................... 14

Blog
It Happened to Me!... 16

Announcement
Protecting the Snowy Plover..................................... 18

Write an Opinion Essay
Should dogs be allowed on the beach? 22

Step 3 • Perform the Task

Should plastic water bottles be banned?

Read Source Materials

Editorial
Ban the Bans on Plastic Water Bottles by Ruth Amnell 28

Infographic
Problems with Plastic 30

Graphic Feature
Out of every 100 plastic bottles made in 2012 32

Write an Opinion Essay
Should plastic water bottles be banned? 35

Unit 2   Informative Essay
The Changing World

Step 1 • Analyze the Model

How do human actions reshape the Earth?

Read Source Materials

Letter
from Enrique 40

Travel Magazine Article
Amazing Sights in Egypt 44

Student Model
Shape Shifting by Hollis Jones 46

© Houghton Mifflin Harcourt Publishing Company • Image Credits: © Picsfive/Shutterstock

Step 2 • Practice the Task

How does erosion change the landscape?

Read Source Materials

Travel Advertisement
Come to Arches National Park 50

Book Review
Yosemite Valley.. 52

Journal Entry
Javier's Diary 54

Write an Opinion Essay
How does erosion change the landscape? 58

Step 3 • Perform the Task

How did a meteor impact affect life on Earth?

Read Source Materials

Science Article
It Came from Outer Space 64

Radio Interview
Why Did Dinosaurs Become Extinct?............................ 66

Question-and-Answer Website
How Did Mammals Survive the K-T Extinction? 68

Write an Informative Essay
How did a meteor impact affect life on Earth?..................... 71

Unit 3 Response to Literature
Courage Comes in All Sizes

Step 1 • Analyze the Model

How can a character show courage?

Read Source Materials

Short Story
Fly Away Home   by Eve Bunting.....................76

Student Model
Calm Courage   by Pilar Pérez 84

Step 2 • Practice the Task

How does a setting influence a character's actions?

Read Source Materials

Excerpt from a Novel
The Girl in the Chicken-Coop   by L. Frank Baum 88

Write a Response to Literature

How does a setting influence a character's actions?................. 98

Step 3 • Perform the Task

What makes a character "larger than life"?

Read Source Materials

Short Story
Lucy de Wilde   by Dina McClellan................................. 104

Write a Response to Literature

What makes a character "larger than life"?........................ 113

Unit 4 Narrative
Wrong Place, Wrong Time

Step 1 • Analyze the Model

What happens to a lone flamingo among swans?

Read Source Materials

Travel Article
Abbotsbury Swannery   by Marcel Smith **118**

Informational Article
The Flamingo   by Jenny Madrid **120**

Student Model
Who's the Ugly Duckling?   by Tanya Wright **122**

Step 2 • Practice the Task

What happens when two schedules get mixed up?

Read Source Materials

Train Schedule
Timetable for North Line **126**

Audition Flyer
Talent Search America **127**

Write a Narrative
What happens when two schedules get mixed up? **130**

Step 3 • Perform the Task

What would happen if you went back in time?

Read Source Materials

Informational Article
Life in Ancient Rome 136

List
What to Pack for My Trip to Rome! 138

Write a Narrative
What would happen if you went back in time? 141

Unit 5 Mixed Practice
On Your Own

TASK 1 • Opinion Essay
Research Simulation

Read Source Materials

Editorial
Handwritten Letters Are Important by Lucida Bright 149

Editorial
Handwritten Letters Belong in the Past by Gill Sans 151

Write an Opinion Essay
Should people send handwritten letters today? 154

TASK 2 • Informative Essay
Research Simulation

Read Source Materials

Informational Article

— —   — — —   • — •   • • •   •

— • — •   — — —   — • •   by Frank Hernandez **159**

Informational Article

The Many Uses of Morse Code   by Peter Hoffman **162**

Write an Informative Essay

How have people used Morse code to communicate? **166**

TASK 3 • Response to Literature

Read Source Materials

Excerpt From A Novel

Ben and Me   by Robert Lawson **171**

Write a Response to Literature

How does Amos's point of view affect his
description of Ben Franklin? **178**

TASK 4 • Narrative
Research Simulation

Read Source Materials

Informational Article

A Shocking Amount of Electricity in Our Lives   by Farrah Diaz **183**

Informational Article

Alternative Energy Sources. **185**

Write a Narrative

What is life like when the electrical grid is shut down? **188**

Eye on the Environment

Opinion Essay

Step 1

Analyze the Model

Evaluate an opinion essay about whether or not people should use disposable bags.

Step 2

Practice the Task

Write an opinion essay about whether or not dogs should be allowed on the beach.

Step 3

Perform the Task

Write an opinion essay about whether or not plastic water bottles should be banned.

When you make a judgment about something, you have an opinion about it. You may feel that the library should be open for longer, or you may think that one song is better than another. Every day, you form opinions. Your friends may not share your opinion about the library or about which song is better.

IN THIS UNIT, you will learn how to write an opinion essay. Your essay will be based on your close reading and examination of sources. You will learn how to state an opinion and give strong reasons that support it. You'll organize your essay in a clear way that makes sense to the reader.

Should people use disposable bags?

You will read:

- **A Magazine Editorial**
  "Reduce" Is the New "Recycle"

- **A Letter to the Editor**
  from Anthony Murray

You will analyze:

- **A Student Model**
  Is Just Recycling Enough?

Source 1: Magazine Editorial

This editorial was used by Mr. Lipsky's student, Taniya Thomas, as one of the sources for her essay, "Is Just Recycling Enough?" As you read, make notes in the side columns. Underline information that you find useful.

Notes

Kind Earth Magazine

"Reduce" Is the New "Recycle"

By Rita Amore, Editor-in-Chief

APRIL 19

Not so long ago, recycling was all the rage. Sorting plastic bottles from the trash was all it took to be thought of as Earth-friendly. Now, however, some experts believe that recycling alone does not solve the problem of pollution. Mark Hader, founder of the organization Stop Buying Now, says recycling "doesn't help as much as we think it does. The best way to stop creating trash and adding to current pollution levels is to stop making new things. Bring your own reusable bag with you when you shop. This would save valuable resources!"

1. **Analyze**   2. Practice   3. Perform

© Houghton Mifflin Harcourt Publishing Company • Image Credits: © Houghton Mifflin Harcourt

Paper bags are made from trees. We only use paper bags for a short time, but it takes many years for one tree to grow. Is it worth cutting down something as beautiful as a tree so that we can use paper bags?

Plastic bags begin as petroleum, a nonrenewable resource. Petroleum is a fossil fuel. When we make bags, we pollute the air and waste fossil fuels. Once we use fossil fuels, they're gone forever. Do we really want to waste them on bags?

So, what's being done to discourage shoppers from using disposable bags? Some cities, including Los Angeles, have banned the use of plastic bags. Shoppers can pay 10¢ for a paper bag, but they won't be offered plastic. Washington, DC, has taxed plastic bags since 2010.

Hopefully, these taxes and bans will encourage our city to take a closer look at our bag policy. We can surely find a way to reduce our bag usage.

Discuss and Decide

What are two ways that cities are reducing disposable bag use? Cite evidence from the article to support your answer.

Source 2: Letter to the Editor

Taniya used this letter to the editor as a second source for her essay. Continue to make notes in the side columns as you read. Underline information that you find helpful.

Notes

Kind Earth Magazine

Letters

Dear Ms. Amore,

I do not think that our city should ban or tax disposable bags. It may seem like the Earth-friendly thing to do, but it's not. Reusable bags can be bad for the environment and for people, too!

Reusable bags aren't meant to last forever. They wear out over time. They may not wear out after only a few uses, but they will eventually wear out. When they can no longer be used, they will end up in the trash, just like a disposable plastic bag.

Creating reusable bags also uses resources. They don't appear out of thin air! An interesting fact that you may not know is that making plastic bags uses less energy than making paper bags. Our city doesn't have a ban or tax on bags, so we can choose plastic. We should choose plastic over paper.

1. **Analyze**   2. Practice   3. Perform

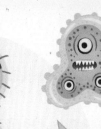

Another fact is that reusable bags can be bad for your health. Germs can stick around for quite awhile in those bags! Some people don't wash their bags, and so germs grow and spread. Gross!

Some people need to know all of the facts before they support a ban or a tax on bags. I think these reusable bags just create problems for customers.

Sincerely,

Anthony Murray, a plastic bag user

Discuss and Decide

You have read two sources about using disposable bags. Without reading any further, discuss the question: Should people use disposable bags?

Analyze a Student Model

Read Taniya's opinion essay closely. The red side notes are the comments that her teacher, Mr. Lipsky, wrote.

Taniya Thomas
December 12

Is Just Recycling Enough?

You state your opinion clearly here. Good work!

Recycling is important, but we need to do more to help the environment. We can reduce what we use. One way we can reduce is by using reusable bags instead of disposable ones.

Great use of academic vocabulary!

We use up <u>resources</u> to make plastic and paper bags. Yes, we use up resources when we make <u>reusable</u> bags once. People buy reusable bags to use again and again. Most people might not use a plastic or paper bag again. Plastic bags are not made to be used many times. They are too thin. They can rip in one trip if you have too many groceries!

Can you combine your ideas on plastic bags into one sentence?

I'd like to see more evidence to support your opinion here.

Some might say that if we recycle paper or plastic bags, there is no problem. But how many people really recycle their disposable bags? We don't know how many people really will recycle the bags they use. It is not always easy to remember to recycle.

1. **Analyze**   2. Practice   3. Perform

Some people say that reusable bags are bad for your health. Germs can grow in them, but only if you don't wash them! Washing these bags seems like a pretty easy thing to do. We can all take the time to wash a bag. We don't have to be lazy!

Good counters to an opposing opinion.

Reusable bags eventually wear out. So does everything else. We can't wear the same clothes forever. But we can use them over and over again before we have to get rid of them. If we reuse our clothes, it makes sense to me to reuse the bags we carry them in, too.

Think about a smoother transition here.

<u>Even if people don't want to use reusable bags, we can make people not want to get disposable bags.</u> Some cities have a tax on bags. If customers take a reusable bag, they have to pay. Why would you want to pay if you can bring your own bag for free? Some cities have bans. They won't let you have a bag, even if you ask! That will stop people from using disposable bags for sure!

This sentence is confusing. How can you clarify?

I'm going to stop using disposable bags, and I hope you do, too!

Discuss and Decide

Does Taniya convince you that reusable bags are worthwhile? If so, cite evidence from her essay that makes you think so. If she doesn't convince you, why not?

Be Clear!

When you write, always check your work. Did you write what you meant to say? In her essay, Taniya could have stated some of her ideas more clearly.

Here is a confusing sentence from Taniya's essay:

> Even if people don't want to use reusable bags, we can make people not want to get disposable bags.

How could Taniya make her ideas clearer? She could state them in a more simple way. Here's an example:

> We can make rules so that people won't want to use disposable bags, even if they did before.

Essay Tips

Remember These Tips When Writing!

- Read a sentence out loud if you are not sure it sounds right. Would your teacher write it the way you wrote it?

- Have a friend look at what you wrote. Does your friend understand what you mean?

Look back through Taniya's essay. Find one sentence that you could improve and underline it. Then rewrite the sentence so that it is more clear. Exchange your work with a partner. Ask your partner if what you wrote is easier to understand than what Taniya wrote.

_____

_____

_____

_____

Should dogs be allowed on the beach?

You will read:

- **A Letter to the Editor**
  from Amanda Evans

- **A Petition**
  from Dog-Owners' Association of Monterey

- **A Blog**
  It Happened to Me!

- **An Announcement**
  Protecting the Snowy Plover

You will write:

- **An Opinion Essay**
  Should dogs be allowed on the beach?

Source 1: Letter to the Editor

AS YOU READ Analyze the letter to the editor. Note information that helps you decide where you stand on the issue: Should dogs be allowed on the beach?

Dog Journal A Magazine for Dog Lovers

Letters

Dear Editor,

I want to thank your magazine for organizing the "Adopt a Dog Day" campaign. It has changed my life and the life of my grandmother!

Grandma is 82 years old and a few months ago she had surgery on both knees. She mostly moved around using her wheelchair. The doctors told her that it would be good for her to walk a bit every day. I tried to get her out for short walks, but she didn't feel like it. She was sad.

Then, one day, I saw that you were going to have "Adopt a Dog Day" in my local park. That's how we found Riley, an adorable dog. Grandma loved Riley!

From that day on, every afternoon, Grandma and I started taking Riley to the beach. At the beginning, Grandma walked slowly and our visits to the beach

1. Analyze   2. Practice   3. Perform

were short. But little by little, she started getting more secure in her walking and our walks were longer and longer.

Now I feel that I got my Grandma back! Thanks to Riley . . . and to *Dog Journal* magazine.

Sincerely,

Amanda Evans

P.S. - Look how happy Grandma is with Riley!

Close Read

Why does Amanda believe dogs should be allowed on the beach? Cite text evidence in your response.

_____

_____

_____

Source 2: Petition

AS YOU READ Analyze the petition. Make notes that help you decide where you stand on the issue: Should dogs be allowed on the beach?

Dog-Owners' Association
of Monterey

98 Vista Avenue, #5
Monterey, CA 93940

The Mayor
City Hall
580 Pacific Ave.
Monterey, CA 93940

Dear Mayor,

We do not agree with the ban of dogs on our local beaches. There are many dog-owners in our community and not enough dog parks. Our dogs need a place to run, exercise, and have fun. Many of us used to take our four-legged friends to one of the beaches nearby until the new law forbade it. Now we don't have a place to take them!

While we understand peoples' concerns, we believe this law is too harsh. There is a way for dogs to enjoy a walk on the beach while keeping members of the

community who don't have pets happy. We think that there is room to compromise.

Most dog owners walk their pets in the morning and in the evening, and not during the hours when the beach would be very busy. As long as we clean up after our dogs, we wouldn't be bothering anybody.

We are respectfully asking you to reconsider, and allow us again to take our dogs to the beach, during off-peak hours.

We've collected over 120 signatures supporting this petition.

Sincerely,

Dog-Owners' Association of Monterey

Close Read

What is the compromise that the Dog-Owners' Association offers the Mayor?

_____

_____

_____

Source 3: Blog

AS YOU READ Analyze the blog. Make notes that help you decide where you stand on the issue: Should dogs be allowed on the beach?

HOME   ABOUT   BLOG LIFE   ARCHIVE

All Things Monterey

A BLOG ABOUT LIFE IN MY BEAUTIFUL TOWN

Saturday, May 31st

Search This Website

It Happened to Me!

Yes, I love dogs. But there's a limit! Here's what happened to me yesterday.

I like to power-walk around the shore each morning, when the beach is deserted and the sun is starting to come out. It's my favorite time of the day, and exercise helps me start the day with positive energy.

Yesterday, I went to the beach, put my headphones on, and started power-walking as small waves crashed softly against my ankles. Great feeling, right? Yes, until my naked feet stepped into a soft, fresh pile of . . . dog you-know-what! Ugh! Disgusting!

Our local laws don't allow dogs on the beach, but some people think that it's OK to take them early in the morning and late in the evening because the dogs don't bother anybody. Maybe. But if you do, CLEAN UP AFTER YOUR DOG!!!

I alerted the local authorities and urged them to increase their presence in the beach area during off-peak hours. They said they'd do their best. We'll see. One thing is for sure—I'm not walking barefoot on the beach any time soon!

Who Is Roger Stevens?

 *I've lived in Monterey all my life. I know many things about this beautiful town and its community, and since people ask me questions about things around town and what's going on all the time, I decided to start this blog. You can subscribe by clicking the button below.*

COMMENTS ❮ 3 ❯

 4 hours ago
young324

You have to calm down, man! It was an accident. No biggie!

 10 hours ago
Knowitall

I agree with you, Roger. If there are no dogs allowed, there shouldn't be exceptions!

 22 hours ago
PuppyAmy

What if the thing you stepped in was brought by the waves?

Sign me up! ♥ Enter your email address: _____

Discuss and Decide
Why did Roger write this blog post?

Source 4: Announcement

AS YOU READ Analyze the announcement. Make notes that help you decide where you stand on the issue: Should dogs be allowed on the beach?

Protecting the Snowy Plover

A Bird in Danger

In March 1993, the western snowy plover was listed as a threatened species, protected under the Endangered Species Act. There are only 2,300 of these birds remaining on the Pacific Coast.

Snowy plovers use sandy beaches for breeding and resting. Their habitat is threatened by urban development, the spread of European dune grass, a higher number of predators in the area, and increased disturbances to their habitats from people and animals.

A snowy plover's natural response is to run or fly from danger. Continuous or repeated disturbance uses up their stored energy reserves and may jeopardize future breeding.

adapted from the **National Park Service**
U.S. Department of the Interior

You Can Help Protect the Snowy Plover

When you are in the snowy plover protection areas, you should:

- Keep your dog on a leash. Snowy plovers perceive dogs as predators.

- Walk, jog, or ride your horse on the wet sand away from the upper parts of the beach where snowy plovers are most likely to be found.

- Fly your kites, and throw balls or flying discs in areas close to the water, away from where snowy plovers rest.

- Dispose of garbage properly to avoid attracting predators.

- Leave kelp and driftwood on the beach—these provide resting and feeding areas for the snowy plover.

For more information, visit http://www.nps.gov/goga/planyourvisit/upload/sb-plight_web.pdf

Discuss and Decide

Why is it important to keep dogs on a leash near snowy plovers? Cite text evidence in your response.

Respond to Questions

These questions will help you analyze the sources you read. Use your notes and refer to the sources in order to answer the questions. Your answers to these questions will help you write your essay.

1 Which source(s) agree that dogs shouldn't be allowed on the beach? How do you know? Make notes about reasons in the chart.

Source	Agrees with the Ban?	Reasons
Letter to the Editor from Amanda Evans	☐ yes ☐ no	
Petition from Dog-Owners' Association of Monterey	☐ yes ☐ no	
Blog It Happened to Me!	☐ yes ☐ no	
Announcement Protecting the Snowy Plover	☐ yes ☐ no	

2 **Prose Constructed-Response** What is one reason why dogs **should** be allowed on the beach? Cite text evidence in your response.

_____

_____

_____

_____

_____

_____

3 **Prose Constructed-Response** What is one reason why dogs **shouldn't** be allowed on the beach? Cite text evidence in your response.

_____

_____

_____

_____

_____

Planning and Prewriting

Before you draft your essay, complete some important planning steps.

Assignment

Write an opinion essay to answer the question: Should dogs be allowed on the beach?

What's Your Opinion?

Think about what you've read and respond below.

 You may prefer to plan on a computer.

Issue: Should dogs be allowed on the beach?

Your position on the issue: ☐ yes ☐ no

Your opinion:

_____

_____

_____

What Are Your Reasons?

Pick three sentences from the sources that helped you form your opinion. Write one sentence in each box below.

Reason	Reason	Reason

Finalize Your Plan

You know what your opinion is on the issue. Now, it's time to plan the structure of your essay. You will save time and create a more organized, logical essay by planning the structure before you start writing.

Use your responses on pages 20–22 to complete the graphic organizer.

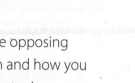

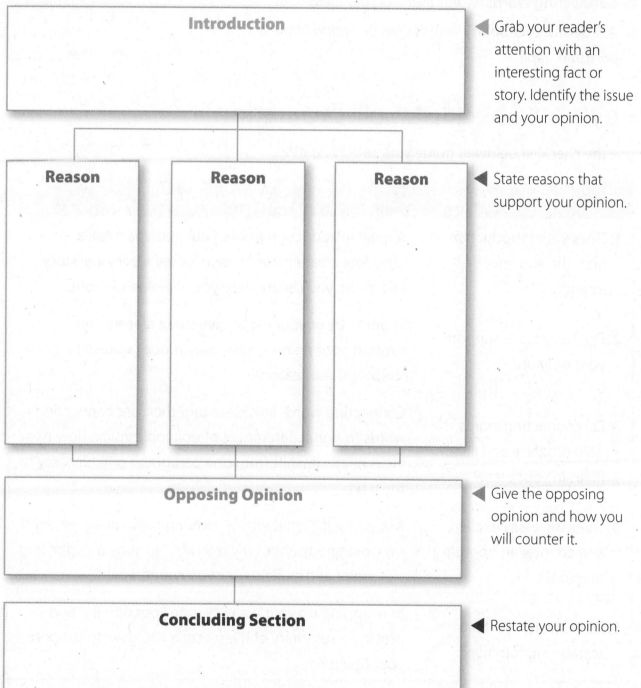

Introduction ◄ Grab your reader's attention with an interesting fact or story. Identify the issue and your opinion.

Reason   **Reason**   **Reason** ◄ State reasons that support your opinion.

Opposing Opinion ◄ Give the opposing opinion and how you will counter it.

Concluding Section ◄ Restate your opinion.

Draft Your Essay

If you drafted your essay on the computer, you may wish to print it out.

As you write, think about:

▶ **Purpose** *what you want to communicate*

▶ **Clarity** *ideas that are straightforward and understandable*

▶ **Support** *examples from the sources that support your opinion*

▶ **Organization** *the logical structure for your essay*

▶ **Connecting Words** *words that link your ideas*

▶ **Academic Vocabulary** *words used in writing about a particular topic*

Revision Checklist: Self-Evaluation

Use the checklist below to guide your self-evaluation.

Ask Yourself	Make It Better
1. Does your introduction grab the audience's attention?	A great introduction hooks your audience. Ask a question, create a vivid image, or tell a personal story. Make sure you clearly state your opinion up front.
2. Do the reasons support your opinion?	In the body of your essay, give three reasons that support your opinion. Give details or examples to support these reasons.
3. Do connecting words help organize and link ideas in your essay?	Connecting words link ideas together. Use connecting words to signal differences of opinion, explain how two ideas relate, or shift from one paragraph of your essay to the next.
4. Does the essay explain and counter an opposing opinion?	Ask yourself, "What would someone who disagrees with my opinion say about my reasons?" Include an opposing viewpoint and explain how you counter it.
5. Does the last section restate your opinion?	In wrapping up your essay, restate your opinion and provide a summary of the reasons you gave to support your opinion.

Revision Checklist: Peer Review

Exchange your essay with a classmate, or read it out loud to your partner. As you read and comment on your partner's essay, focus on organization and evidence. You do not need to agree with your partner's opinion. Help your partner find parts of the draft that need to be revised.

What To Look For	Notes for My Partner
1. Does the introduction grab the audience's attention?	
2. Do the reasons support the stated opinion?	
3. Do connecting words help organize and link ideas in the essay?	
4. Does the essay explain and counter an opposing opinion?	
5. Does the last section restate the opinion?	

Use Connecting Words

Review Your Use of Connecting Words

To make your essay read smoothly and to link your ideas, use connecting words. Connecting words show how two things or ideas are related.

These sentences are choppy and interrupt the flow of ideas:

> The plovers do not nest on the beach. The plovers do spend ten months there.

This sentence is smooth and links both ideas together:

> Although the plovers do not nest on the beach, they do spend ten months there.

Essay Tips

Use Connecting Words!

Here are some connecting words that you might use when you revise your essay.

although	even though	in addition
because	for example	since
but	for instance	therefore
even if	in order to	while

Edit

Edit your essay to correct spelling, grammar, and punctuation errors.

Should plastic water bottles be banned?

You will read:

- **An Editorial**
  Ban the Bans on Plastic Water Bottles

- **An Infographic**
  Problems with Plastic

- **A Graphic Feature**
  Out of Every 100 Plastic Bottles Made in 2012 . . .

You will write:

- **An Opinion Essay**
  Should plastic water bottles be banned?

AS YOU READ

Look for reasons that support your opinion, or reasons that make you change your opinion about this question: Should plastic water bottles be banned?

Notes

Ban the Bans on Plastic Water Bottles

By Ruth Amnell

Plastic water bottles are a necessary part of modern life. They are the easiest way to access water when we're on the go. But they're getting a bad reputation. The town of Concord, Massachusetts, has even banned the sale of some types of plastic bottles. Environmentalists want to get rid of plastic bottles, but they might see things differently if they consider the points below.

People in favor of plastic bottle bans say that we
10 can get water from water fountains. When was the last time you saw a water fountain? It's probably been a long time. Water fountains are a thing of the past. If you want a sip of water while you're out, don't expect to find a water fountain.

Even if you could find a water fountain, you wouldn't want to drink from it! Water fountains are covered in germs. People put their mouths on the spout, spreading whatever germs they might have. The bacteria that collects can make people sick.
20 Why take that chance when you can use a water bottle? Grabbing a plastic water bottle before you leave the house can help you avoid these germ-filled sources of water.

Some parts of the world don't have clean water to drink. If you are traveling to a place where the water isn't safe to drink, a plastic water bottle is the best way to get water. You could boil the water, but only if you have access to a stove. How likely is that? When health is involved, you don't want to risk

30   drinking water that isn't safe.

If water bottles are banned from indoor and outdoor events, other healthy drink options need to be made available. Most of these bans are directed at plastic bottles that contain water, but the bans don't apply to plastic soda bottles! If you want to buy a beverage from a food truck vendor, for example, soda will be the only option. If you don't want to drink soda, you're out of luck.

What about the chemicals in plastic water

40   bottles? Yes, there are some. But there are no cases of people getting sick from those chemicals. There are chemicals in many items that we use every day. So don't worry about it!

Plastic water bottle bans have not been adopted by many cities yet. Perhaps, if the decision to ban these bottles is carefully considered, no other cities will institute the ban.

Close Read

What example supports the author's point about needing plastic water bottles at indoor and outdoor events?

Source 2: Infographic

Problems with Plastic

Where does the water in bottled water actually come from? The pictures of mountains and fresh lakes on some water bottles may make us think that the water in those bottles comes from these places, but that may not be the case. The water in your plastic bottle may actually be tap water. Here are some other bottled water facts.

Plastic bottles can take many hundreds of years to break down.

In 2009, Bundanoon, a city in Australia, became the first city in the world to ban bottled water from stores. Water fountains were put up around the city.

In 2013, Concord, Massachusetts became the first town in the United States to ban plastic water bottles.

1. Analyze   2. Practice   3. Perform

It takes three liters of water to produce each one-liter bottle of water.

22% of bottled water brands tested contained chemicals above state health limits.

In 2011, sales of bottled water in the United States totaled $21.7 billion.

Americans buy 29 billion bottles of water a year.

A 60-watt light bulb can be powered for six hours with the energy saved from recycling one plastic bottle.

For every six water bottles we use, only one is recycled. The rest are sent to landfills.

Discuss and Decide

What effects do plastic bottles have on the environment?

Source 3: Graphic Feature

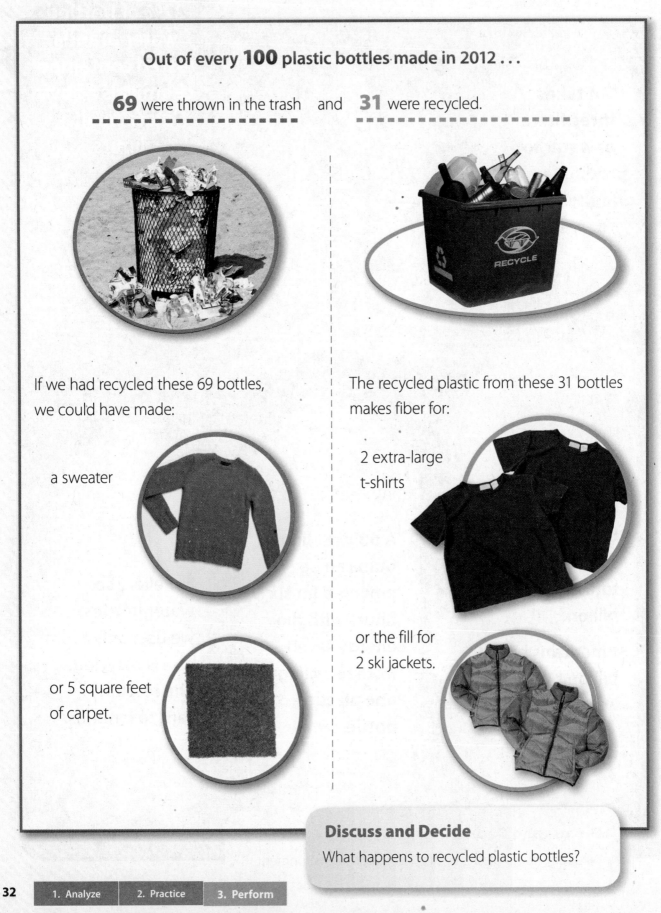

Out of every 100 plastic bottles made in 2012 . . .

69 were thrown in the trash   and   **31** were recycled.

If we had recycled these 69 bottles, we could have made:

a sweater

or 5 square feet of carpet.

The recycled plastic from these 31 bottles makes fiber for:

2 extra-large t-shirts

or the fill for 2 ski jackets.

Discuss and Decide

What happens to recycled plastic bottles?

Respond to Questions

These questions will help you think about the sources you've read. Use your notes and refer to the sources to answer the questions. Your answers to these questions will help you write your essay.

1 According to the sources, which of the following is a reason to ban bottled water?

   a. There are chemicals in plastic water bottles. (Source 1)

   b. Plastic water bottles can help you avoid drinking unsafe water. (Source 1)

   c. Some bottled water is tap water. (Source 2)

   d. In 2012, 31% of plastic bottles were recycled. (Source 3)

2 According to Source 1, why should people avoid using water fountains?

   a. The water that comes from fountains is dirty.

   b. Water fountains have been banned in some cities.

   c. Bacteria can collect on water fountains.

   d. There are harmful chemicals in water fountains.

3 Which sentence best supports your answer to Question 2?

   a. "People put their mouths on the spout, spreading whatever germs they might have." (lines 17–18)

   b. "When health is involved, you don't want to risk drinking water that isn't safe." (lines 29–30)

   c. "If you don't want to drink soda, you're out of luck." (lines 37–38)

   d. "There are chemicals in many items that we use every day." (lines 41–42)

4 Which sentence best supports the idea that banning plastic water bottles may have harmful consequences?

a. "When health is involved, you don't want to risk drinking water that isn't safe." (Source 1)

b. "Plastic water bottle bans have not been adopted by many cities yet." (Source 1)

c. "Plastic bottles can take many hundreds of years to break down." (Source 2)

d. "The recycled plastic from these 31 bottles makes fiber for 2 extra-large t-shirts." (Source 3)

5 Which source(s) agree that plastic water bottles should be banned? How do you know? Record your reasons in the chart.

Source	Agrees with the Ban?		Reasons
Editorial Ban the Bans on Plastic Water Bottles	☐ yes	☐ no	
Infographic Problems with Plastic	☐ yes	☐ no	
Graphic Feature "Out of every 100 plastic bottles made in 2012 . . . "	☐ yes	☐ no	

6 **Prose-Constructed Response** What information in Source 3 can support the writer's opinion on plastic water bottles in Source 1? Cite evidence from the text in your response.

_____

_____

_____

Write the Essay

Read the assignment.

Plan

Use the graphic organizer to help you outline the structure of your opinion essay.

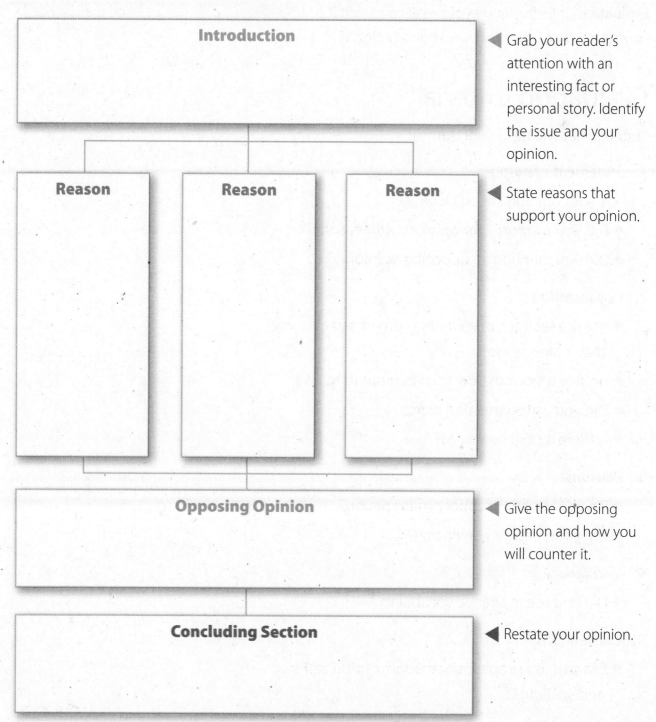

Introduction — Grab your reader's attention with an interesting fact or personal story. Identify the issue and your opinion.

Reason | **Reason** | **Reason** — State reasons that support your opinion.

Opposing Opinion — Give the opposing opinion and how you will counter it.

Concluding Section — Restate your opinion.

Draft

Use your notes and completed graphic organizer
to write a first draft of your opinion essay.

Revise and Edit

Look back over your essay and compare it to the
Evaluation Criteria. Revise your essay and edit it to
correct spelling, grammar, and punctuation errors.

You may wish to
draft and edit your essay
on the computer.

Evaluation Criteria

Your teacher will be looking for:

1. **Statement of purpose**
   - Is your opinion stated clearly?
   - Did you support your opinion with reasons?
   - Did you mention an opposing opinion?

2. **Organization**
   - Are the sections of your essay organized in a way
     that makes sense?
   - Is there a smooth flow from beginning to end?
   - Did you use connecting words?
   - Is there a clear conclusion?

3. **Reasons**
   - Do your reasons support your opinion?
   - Are your reasons convincing?

4. **Vocabulary**
   - Did you use academic vocabulary?

5. **Conventions**
   - Did you use proper punctuation, capitalization,
     and spelling?

The Changing World

Informative Essay

Step 1

Analyze the Model

Evaluate an informative essay about the ways human actions reshape the Earth.

Step 2

Practice the Task

Write an informative essay about changes to the physical world caused by wind, water, and ice.

Step 3

Perform the Task

Write an informative essay about the effects of a meteor impact on Earth.

An informative essay is a short piece of writing that informs and explains. It is nonfiction, and deals with real people, events, and places without changing any facts. Informative writing includes newspapers, magazines, and online articles, as well as biographies, speeches, movie and book reviews, and true-life adventure stories.

The sources in this unit discuss various actions that change our planet—human projects, natural processes, and devastating events. The information in these texts is factual.

IN THIS UNIT, you will evaluate the way writers organize their informative essays, and analyze information from nonfiction articles, maps, and photographs. Then you will use what you have learned to write informative essays of your own.

How do human actions reshape the Earth?

You will read:

- **A Letter**
  from Enrique

- **A Travel Magazine Article**
  Amazing Sights in Egypt

You will analyze:

- **A Student Model**
  Shape Shifting

Source 1: Letter

The following letter was used by Ms. Garcia's student, Hollis Jones, as one of her sources for an essay answering the question "How do human actions reshape the Earth?" As you read, make notes in the side columns. Underline information that you find helpful.

Notes

November 12

Hey Marcelo,

You wanted some ideas for your assignment on great engineering achievements. So, here goes!

First up is something you've probably heard of—the Panama Canal. This is a man-made waterway in Central America that connects the Atlantic and Pacific oceans. Before the canal, a ship traveling between New York and San Francisco had to sail 13,000 miles, around the tip of South America. The canal reduced the length of the voyage to 5,000 miles.

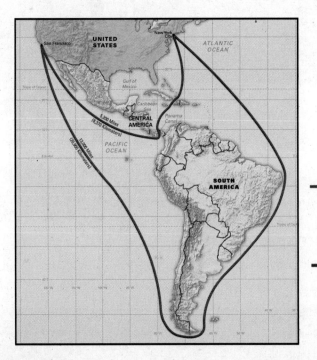

— New York City to San Francisco, around South America

— New York City to San Francisco, through Panama Canal

The canal crosses land that is not flat. To deal with the change in height above sea level, locks raise the level of the water 85 feet. They can even lift giant warships. Today, about 15,000 ships pass through the Panama Canal every year.

Some numbers help show what a huge undertaking it was to build the 51-mile-long canal. About 30,000 tons of dynamite were used to excavate about 200 million cubic yards of material. The job cost nearly 9 billion dollars in today's money, and about 25,000 workers died from disease and accidents.

Panama Canal

The Panama Canal was built because land got in the way of two oceans. But how about when water gets in the way of two pieces of land? The Tsugaru Strait is a body of water between the Japanese islands of Honshu and Hokkaido. After a storm sank several ferries crossing the strait, the Japanese decided to build a train tunnel to connect the islands. The Seikan Tunnel is the longest train tunnel in the world. It stretches 33 miles, and 14 miles of it is more than 300 feet below the sea bed. There are even two underwater stations—the world's first.

People have even made land where there was only water before. Dubai has only about 40 miles of natural coastline. To encourage tourism, the state built the Palm Jumeirah island. The island is connected to the mainland by a bridge, and extends nearly three and a half miles into the Persian Gulf. It is shaped like a palm tree surrounded by a 7-mile-long crescent, and gives Dubai another 42 miles of beachfront. Over 100 million cubic yards of sand and 7 million tons of rock was used

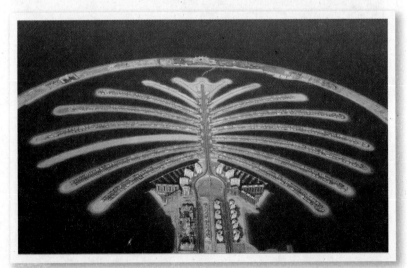

Palm Jumeriah Island

Battery Park City

to build the island. Apparently, that is enough material to build a wall ten feet tall and one foot wide, circling the world three times!

Palm Jumeirah isn't the only major example of new land. Battery Park City, at the southern end of Manhattan, is built on a landfill! That doesn't mean it's a cheap place to live. Right now, the average rent for an apartment there is almost $4,000 a month.

Hope these examples help!

Your big brother, to the rescue again,

Enrique

Close Read

According to the letter, what are some of the reasons that people make major changes to their surroundings?

Source 2: Travel Magazine Article

Hollis used this magazine article as a second source for her essay. Continue to make notes in the side columns as you read. Underline information that you find helpful.

Notes

Amazing Sights in Egypt

In the middle of the desert, 500 miles south of Cairo, is a huge structure that took 30,000 workers ten years to build. This is the Aswan High Dam, an engineering marvel. It's 364 feet tall and more than two miles long.

The Aswan High Dam holds back the River Nile, forming a reservoir, Lake Nasser. The lake is 300 miles long and averages 14 miles across. You can fish there, and watch an amazing variety of birds. More than 100 species live or migrate over the lake. Just don't swim near its sandy shores. Lake Nasser is also home to about 70,000 crocodiles!

However, fishing and bird watching were not at the top of the list of reasons for building the dam. The River Nile floods every year. Once the dam was

1. Analyze   2. Practice   3. Perform

completed in 1970, people could control the water. When there is too much water, the dam holds it back. In times of drought, water is released from the reservoir to farmlands downstream. The dam also generates an enormous amount of electricity.

Egypt is the site of one of the world's earliest civilizations. The area that was flooded to form Lake Nasser was home to many important buildings from thousands of years ago. The most famous are the two Abu Simbel temples, carved into the face of a tall cliff. The outside of the larger temple has four seated figures that are each 67 feet tall. The temples were painstakingly dismantled, and a new mountain was built on higher ground. There, the temples were carefully rebuilt. This engineering feat is nearly as amazing as the building of the dam itself.

If you're ever in New York City, you can see a smaller temple that was saved from rising waters of Lake Nasser. The Temple of Dendur was given to the United States by the government of Egypt. It now has its own pavilion in the Metropolitan Museum of Art.

Discuss and Decide

Why did Egypt build the Aswan High Dam? Cite text evidence in your response.

Analyze a Student Model

Hollis wrote an essay that answered the question: How do human actions reshape the Earth? The red notes are the comments that her teacher, Ms. Garcia, wrote.

Hollis Jones

January 22

Shape Shifting

Good, clear opening.

People often change their surroundings to improve their lives. Someone might dig a foundation to build a house or level some land to plant a lawn. But sometimes the changes that people make are on a scale that is hard to imagine.

This is a great observation!

Huge engineering projects have changed the shape of our world in a big way. Many of these changes involve water. We dig under the sea, we connect bodies of water, we replace water with land, and we contain water.

In Japan, the Seikan Tunnel was built to provide a safer way to travel between two islands. It is the longest underwater train tunnel in the world and makes its way 300 feet below the sea bed.

The Panama Canal is only 51 miles long, but it connects two oceans! It cuts about 8,000 miles from the sea voyage around South America. Digging a

canal that can handle big ships was a massive project. The amount of land that was moved, the dynamite used to do it, and the cost in money and workers' lives are mind-blowing.

People build islands, too! In the Persian Gulf, there is an island where there used to be only water. Using enough sand and rock to build a tall wall that would stretch three times around the Earth, Dubai built an island shaped like a palm tree. The edges of each leaf provide beachfront as an attraction for tourists.

The problem of having too much water or too little water can sometimes be solved by building a dam. In Egypt, the Aswan High Dam stops the Nile from flooding the land, and it releases water when there is a drought. It's over two miles long, and it took 30,000 workers ten years to complete.

All of these projects changed the shape of the Earth. Each one took a huge amount of time, money, and work. And each one accomplished its purpose: to improve life.

Use a more formal word or phrase for "mind-blowing"?

You've organized the different examples in a clear way.

Nice concluding paragraph!

Discuss and Decide

What is Hollis's main idea? Did she choose appropriate examples from the sources to support her main idea?

Organizing an Informative Essay

In "Shape Shifting," Hollis used a main-idea-and-details organization. She presented her main idea in the first paragraph, and then supported the idea with details in the paragraphs that follow. Hollis summed up her main idea in the concluding paragraph.

Complete the chart below with examples from Hollis's essay.

Introduction

◄ The first paragraph introduces the main idea of the essay. It usually includes an interesting detail, question, or idea.

Detail

◄ The following paragraphs support the main idea with details and examples.

Detail

Detail

Conclusion

◄ The final paragraph often restates the main idea, and includes a further insight or observation.

1. Analyze   2. Practice   3. Perform

How does erosion change the landscape?

You will read:

- **A Travel Advertisement**
  Come to Arches National Park

- **A Book Review**
  Yosemite Valley

- **A Journal Entry**
  Javier's Diary

You will write:

- **An Informative Essay**
  How does erosion change the landscape?

Source 1: Travel Advertisement

AS YOU READ You will be writing an informative essay that explains how erosion changes the landscape. As you read the advertisement, underline and circle information that you may cite as textual evidence when you write your essay.

Come to Arches National Park

Up in the high desert of Utah is the world's greatest collection of natural arches. And now's the time to visit! If you had come millions of years ago, all you would have seen was a flat layer of rock that extended a mile above what is now Arches National Park.

The amazing landscape at Arches was sculpted by time, water, and wind. Erosion has formed over 2,000 sandstone arches, along with spires, domes, fins, pinnacles, and hoodoos. In case you're wondering, a hoodoo is a rock formation that looks a bit like a totem pole. It's a thin spire topped with a larger, harder rock that is less

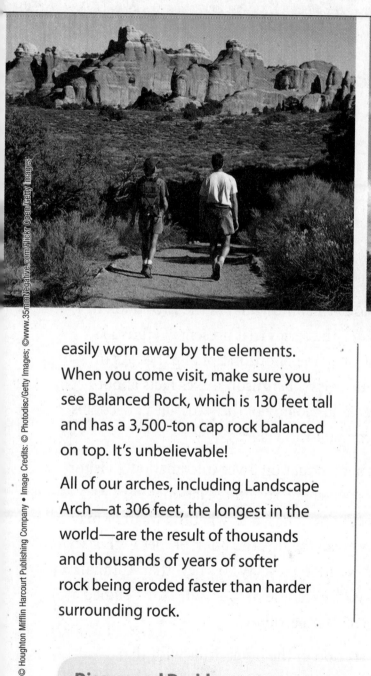

easily worn away by the elements. When you come visit, make sure you see Balanced Rock, which is 130 feet tall and has a 3,500-ton cap rock balanced on top. It's unbelievable!

All of our arches, including Landscape Arch—at 306 feet, the longest in the world—are the result of thousands and thousands of years of softer rock being eroded faster than harder surrounding rock.

So take the time to come and see some of nature's most dramatic marvels. And take note: Wall Arch collapsed in 2008. Come soon, before they are all gone.*

*We're kidding! While some arches may fall during the next 50 years, there will be plenty left, and more will be slowly forming.

Discuss and Decide

How does erosion create rock formations such as Landscape Arch?

Source 2: Book Review

AS YOU READ Analyze the book review. As you read, continue to underline and circle information that you may cite as textual evidence when you write your essay.

Black Ink Review • April 23

Yosemite Valley
by Raindrop Ferguson

Yosemite Valley is the fifth book in the series that presents Ferguson's reflections on some of our national parks. As in his previous works, Ferguson mixes facts about the geology and biology of the park with anecdotes about its rangers and visitors.

The book's introduction gives information a visitor needs, such as where Yosemite National Park is, what rules the park has, and what the weather may be like. Ferguson begins the book proper with a brief history of the park. Who knew that Abraham Lincoln—in the middle of the Civil War—signed a grant protecting the valley?

The next section of the book deals with the geological formation of Yosemite Valley. It turns out that rocks carried by glaciers gouged the valley into a U-shape with steep walls. Glacial erosion also created the spectacular domes and peaks of the park, and rocks deposited by the glaciers when they retreated created a natural dam, forming the old Lake Yosemite, which is now a meadow. Glaciers also carved gorges high above the valley floor. Once the ice was gone, some of these gorges became river beds, feeding Yosemite's stunning waterfalls.

In the final section, Ferguson's hikes through the Wilderness (95% of the park) informed his descriptions of the plants and animals of the park, including an amusing encounter with a black bear.

This short work combines the best of a guidebook, historical account, geology primer, and friendly chat. It's the most readable of Ferguson's national parks books so far.

Close Read

How did the waterfalls form in Yosemite National Park?

_____

_____

_____

Source 3: Journal Entry

AS YOU READ Analyze the journal entry. As you read, continue to underline and circle information that you may cite as textual evidence when you write your essay.

Javier's Diary

Bright Angel Trail

June 11, 2014 —

It's my birthday, but I got up at 5:30 this morning. There was something I wanted to do!

Dad and I had a quick bite and packed the things we needed: three bottles of water each, a lot of salty snacks, sandwiches, hats, and sunscreen. Dad had a first aid kit, and we both had cameras. We set off to the head of the Bright Angel Trail down into the Grand Canyon. We weren't the only ones hiking, but it was still exciting. Within ten minutes, we reached a tunnel that was cut through the canyon wall. This hole was made by people, not erosion. But the rest of the canyon was formed by the Colorado River over millions of years. Rushing water carved out the mile-deep, 277-mile-long canyon. When I first learned that, I thought it was weird, but then I thought about the way the ocean changes the coastline. Just water.

After about a mile, the trail got steeper, but it was still a pretty easy stroll. Glad I wore hiking boots, though. The crowd started to thin out, and the views were great. Some of the rock formations at the top of the canyon have been eroded by wind (carrying sand) and there are great shapes.

Soon we reached another tunnel, and it got a bit steeper as the path ran along high cliff edges. We made it to a rest house that's about a mile and a half from the top, and stopped for some food and more water. It was still early, but we didn't want to be out in the scorching sun later on. A few people were starting to come up the trail from the bottom of the canyon, and they had the right of way. So did a mule train that was carrying supplies down the trail.

Mule train

Dad and I walked until we got to the 3 Mile Rest House, at about 8 o'clock. And ate lunch! The rest house was really four piles of rocks with a roof on it, but it was good to sit in the shade there. We rested for a while and refilled our water bottles. I wanted to keep going, but Dad's knees were starting to bother him, and he pointed out that the trail would seem steeper going up than it had coming down.

Dad was right! The trip back up took quite a bit longer, and we were both pretty exhausted when we got back to the canyon rim at about 11:30. We both have great photos from our hike, which I'm going to look at a lot to remind myself of what an amazing day (or morning) I had.

Heading back!

Discuss and Decide

How were the rock formations created at the top of the canyon?

Respond to Questions

The following questions will help you think about the sources you've read. Use your notes and refer to the sources as you answer the questions. Your answers will help you write your essay.

1 Which of the following statements is true according to the information in Source 1?

 a. Arches National Park hasn't changed in millions of years.

 b. Each arch in the park takes a million years to form.

 c. The arches did not exist a million years ago.

 d. Arches National Park has about a million rock formations.

2 How did glaciers form Yosemite Valley?

 a. Ice melted into the rock and then froze, breaking the rock.

 b. Rocks that the glaciers dragged with them eroded the valley.

 c. The force of the ice wall pushed everything out of the way.

 d. The glaciers formed a lake that then drained.

3 Which detail from Source 2 best supports your answer to Question 2?

 a. "Glacial erosion also created the spectacular domes and peaks ..."

 b. "... rocks deposited by the glaciers when they retreated created a natural dam ..."

 c. "... rocks carried by glaciers gouged the valley into a U-shape ..."

 d. "... some of these gorges became river beds, feeding Yosemite's stunning waterfalls."

④ How was the Grand Canyon formed?

    a. Currents sculpted it when it was under the ocean.

    b. Heavy winds for millions of years wore away the soft rock.

    c. It was a natural lake that drained thousands of years ago.

    d. Over millions of years, the Colorado River carved the canyon into the land.

⑤ In what way are hoodoos similar to arches?

    a. Hoodoos are what is left when arches collapse.

    b. They are both formed of rocks that erode at different rates.

    c. Both hoodoos and arches are more than 130 feet tall.

    d. They are both formed from boulders left by glaciers.

⑥ **Prose Constructed-Response** What formed the waterfalls that tumble down the walls of Yosemite National Park? List the causes and their effects. Cite text evidence from Source 2 in your response.

_____

_____

_____

⑦ **Prose Constructed-Response** What is one reason that all of the places mentioned in the sources were made national parks? Cite text evidence from each source.

_____

_____

_____

_____

Planning and Prewriting

Before you begin to write an informative essay, you need to determine how you will organize it. The assignment asks you to answer a question that includes the words *how* and *change*. These words suggest that you might write a cause-and-effect essay. Cause-and-effect writing explains the reason something (or more than one thing) happens.

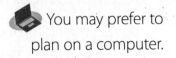 You may prefer to plan on a computer.

Collect Information

When you include information from a source in your writing, only use material that applies to your topic. Don't include extra information—it would make your essay confusing and distract the reader from your main point.

Complete the chart with information you'll use from each source.

Source	Evidence from Source	Cause and Effect
Travel Advertisement Come to Arches National Park		
Book Review Yosemite Valley		
Journal Entry Javier's Diary		

1. Analyze   2. Practice   3. Perform

Finalize Your Plan

Use your responses and notes from previous pages to make a plan for your essay.

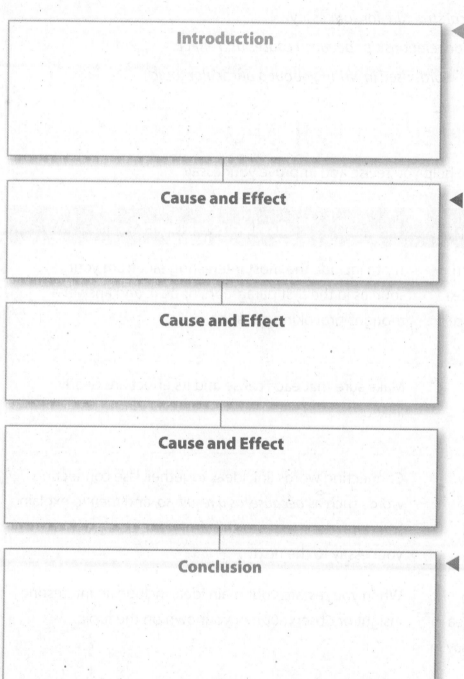

Introduction

The first paragraph presents an overall look at the main causes and effects in the essay. It often includes an interesting detail, question, or idea.

Cause and Effect

The following paragraphs provide details that explain and support the ideas in your introduction.

Cause and Effect

Cause and Effect

Conclusion

The final paragraph often restates the overall causes and effects, and includes a further insight or observation.

Draft Your Essay

If you drafted your essay on the computer, you may wish to print it out.

As you write, think about:

▶ **Purpose** *to use sources to write a cause-and-effect essay*

▶ **Audience** *your teacher and your classmates*

▶ **Organization** *the logical structure for your essay*

▶ **Clarity** *easily understood relationships between causes and effects*

▶ **Academic Vocabulary** *words used in writing about a particular topic*

Revision Checklist: Self-Evaluation

Use the checklist below to help you revise and improve your essay.

Ask Yourself	Revision Strategies
1. Does the introduction present your main idea and grab the audience's attention?	Try to include the most interesting fact from your sources in the first paragraph, or pose and answer a thought-provoking question.
2. Is the relationship between causes and effects clear?	Make sure that each cause and its effect are clearly linked.
3. Does your essay flow well and connect the details to the overall idea?	Connecting words link ideas together. Use connecting words such as *because, as a result, so,* and *then* to explain how two ideas relate or shift from one paragraph of your essay to the next.
4. Does the conclusion restate your main idea and wrap up the essay in an interesting way?	When you restate your main idea, include an interesting insight or observation of your own on the topic.

Revision Checklist: Peer Review

Exchange your essay with a classmate. Read and comment on your partner's essay, focusing on how well it explains how erosion changes the landscape.

Help your partner find parts of the draft that could be improved.

What to Look For	Notes for My Partner
1. Does the introduction present the main idea and grab the audience's attention?	
2. Is the relationship between causes and effects clear?	
3. Does the essay flow well and connect the details to the main idea?	
4. Does the conclusion restate the main idea and wrap up the essay in an interesting way?	

Revision: Writing an Introduction

The best way to make readers interested in your work is to capture their attention! One way to grab a reader's attention is to include a fascinating fact in your first paragraph. You'll need to connect the fact to your main idea.

This introduction gets the reader's attention with a question and interesting answer, and states the point of the essay:

> What could cut a gash through rock nearly 300 miles long and one mile deep? Over a long period of time, water could do it! That's how the Grand Canyon was formed. Water, wind, and ice can change the landscape in amazing ways.

Essay Tips

Attention-Getting Advice

- Write a statement that makes the reader want to find out more.

- Use an interesting, thought-provoking quote.

- Present a fact that will shock or surprise the reader.

- Write a brief account of a fascinating event.

- Ask a question that the reader can relate to.

Edit

Edit your essay to correct spelling, grammar, and punctuation errors.

How did a meteor impact affect life on Earth?

You will read:

- **A Science Article**
  It Came from Outer Space

- **A Radio Interview**
  Why Did Dinosaurs Become Extinct?

- **A Question-and-Answer Website**
  How Did Mammals Survive the K-T Extinction?

You will write:

- **An Informative Essay**
  How did a meteor impact affect life on Earth?

Source 1: Science Article

AS YOU READ
You will be writing a cause-and-effect informative essay that explains how a meteor impact affected life on Earth. As you read the sources, underline information that you may cite as textual evidence in your essay.

Notes

It Came from Outer Space

by Jane Park

In 1981, two scientists uncovered an element called iridium in the ground in Italy. Iridium is rare on Earth, so they thought it must have come from space, where it is more common. They dated the iridium to 65 million years ago.

Ten years later, scientists found that a crater called Chicxulub (CHEEK-she-loob) in Mexico was formed 65 million years
10 ago. Chicxulub is 110 miles across and almost a mile deep. If iridium reached Earth 65 million years ago, maybe the crater was formed by a huge object from space.

United States

Gulf of Mexico

Mexico

Chicxulub Crater

Yucatán

Here's what happened. A meteor measuring more than six miles across and weighing over 1,000,000,000,000 tons hit Earth at a speed of 40,000 miles per hour,

20 times as fast as a bullet. An object that huge
traveling that fast has an enormous amount of
20   energy. On impact, it released as much energy as
100 trillion tons of TNT! The explosion of hot rock
and gas would have looked like a huge fireball.

A lot of that energy turned into heat. It scorched
the surface of the earth and started wildfires across
the world. Debris scattered all across the western
hemisphere. It turned the sky black and blocked out
the sun, starting a winter that lasted for years. So
much debris in the air caused poisonous acid rain
to fall, too. The impact caused earthquakes and
30   mile-high tsunamis across all of what is now North
and South America.

Many scientists believe that it also spelled
the end of the dinosaurs.

Discuss and Decide

How is the presence of iridium on Earth connected to the
Chicxulub Crater? Cite text evidence in your discussion.

Why Did Dinosaurs Become Extinct?

Mike DeMarco: Welcome back to Dino Discussion. Our guest today is Dr. Tara Nadon, a scientist at the National Dinosaur Center. Thank you for joining us, Dr. Nadon. Dinosaurs roamed the earth for over 150 million years. But then they went extinct. Can you tell us about the extinction and why it happened?

Dr. Nadon: Thanks for having me on the show. Scientists call that extinction the Cretaceous-Tertiary event, or K-T event for short. It happened about 65 million years ago. We don't know exactly why it happened, but many scientists think a meteor that hit the Yucatán Peninsula at around the same time played a huge part.

Mike DeMarco: What effects would that meteor have had on dinosaurs?

Dr. Nadon: It wasn't just the dinosaurs that were affected. Any plants or animals near where the meteor hit would have been killed instantly by the explosion or broiled alive by the incredible heat given off. Then acid rain and wildfires would have killed most of the life that survived the impact. What's more, all the dust kicked into the air blocked out the sun for many years. This killed most plant species because they needed the sun to make food for themselves.

© Houghton Mifflin Harcourt Publishing Company • Image Credits: ©Guy Jarvis/Houghton Mifflin Harcourt

Mike DeMarco: But clearly not all life went extinct, or else we wouldn't be here right now. Why the dinosaurs?

Dr. Nadon: Well, many dinosaurs were large creatures that needed a lot of food to survive. When all the plants died due to the lack of sunlight, plant-eating dinosaurs starved to death. Then the dinosaurs that ate those plant-eating dinosaurs died, too, because they had nothing left to eat.

Mike DeMarco: I see. So the effects went all the way up the food chain.

Dr. Nadon: That's right. Also, most dinosaurs had very specific diets, so they couldn't adapt when their food sources disappeared.

Mike DeMarco: It's incredible that anything could adapt in such a harsh environment. Thanks for your time today, Dr. Nadon.

Close Read

Explain how the effects of the meteor impact "went all the way up the food chain." Cite text evidence in your response..

_____

_____

_____

Source 3: Question-and-Answer Website

Science & Mathematics > Zoology

Search This Website

User johnnie1337 asked:

How Did Mammals Survive the K-T Extinction?

Best Answer (Asker's Choice)

User dinofan65:

After the meteor hit, some small mammals survived by burrowing underground. Others escaped to rivers or the oceans.

A lack of sunlight killed many of the land plants that herbivorous dinosaurs ate. When the herbivores died, the carnivorous dinosaurs had nothing to eat, either. But many small mammals were scavengers, eating all types of plants, insects, and even the remains of dead animals. Underwater plants and insects survived fairly well, so the mammals had a food supply.

Mammals took over roles in the environment that used to be filled by dinosaurs. They had lots of babies, too, so their numbers grew quickly.

Some mammals probably survived just because they were lucky or in the right place at the right time.

Asker's rating & comment   👍 Like   👎 Dislike

✳✳✳✳✳

Thanks!

Discuss and Decide

What are two reasons mammals survived the K-T Extinction while dinosaurs didn't?

Respond to Questions

The following questions will help you think about the sources you've read. Use your notes and refer to the sources as you answer the questions. Your answers will help you write the essay.

1 Which detail in Source 2 best explains why plant-eating dinosaurs went extinct?

   a. "... acid rain and wildfires would have killed most of the life ..."

   b. "... all the plants died due to the lack of sunlight ..."

   c. "... animals near where the meteor hit would have been killed instantly ..."

   d. "... most dinosaurs had very specific diets ..."

2 Which detail in Source 1 best describes the force with which the meteor hit the Yucatan Peninsula?

   a. "... it released as much energy as 100 trillion tons of TNT!"

   b. "... a crater called Chicxulub in Mexico was formed 65 million years ago."

   c. "So much debris in the air caused poisonous acid rain to fall, too."

   d. "A lot of that energy turned into heat."

3 What is the best meaning for *debris* as it is used in lines 25 and 28 of "It Came from Outer Space"?

   a. heat and light

   b. energy

   c. cold

   d. dirt and rocks

④ Which of the following is a claim you could make after reading the sources?

   a. One of the ways mammals survived the meteor impact was by eating dinosaurs.

   b. The sky turning black killed only plant-eating dinosaurs.

   c. The fact that mammals were picky eaters helped them survive.

   d. The extinction of the dinosaurs allowed mammals to fill more roles in the environment.

⑤ **Prose Constructed-Response** What are some reasons that the meteor had such a great effect when it hit Earth? Cite details from "It Came from Outer Space" in your response.

_____

_____

_____

_____

⑥ **Prose Constructed-Response** Look at the interview in Source 2 and the post in Source 3. How do they work together to give you a better understanding of how mammals managed to survive the K-T Extinction? Cite text evidence in your response.

_____

_____

_____

_____

_____

Write the Essay

Read the assignment.

Plan

Use the graphic organizer to help you outline the structure of your informative essay.

Assignment
You have read about a meteor impact that happened 65 million years ago. Write an informative essay about how this meteor impact affected life on Earth. Cite text evidence from what you have read.

Introduction

◀ State your main idea. Include an interesting detail, question, or quotation to hook your audience. Identify the causes and effects you will be writing about.

Cause and Effect

◀ Organize your causes and effects in a way that makes sense. Each paragraph should give details that support the ideas you presented in the introduction.

Cause and Effect

Cause and Effect

Conclusion

◀ Restate your overall idea and try to include a further insight or observation.

Draft

Use your notes and completed graphic organizer to write a first draft of your informational essay.

Revise and Edit

Look back over your essay and compare it to the Evaluation Criteria. Revise your essay and edit it to correct spelling, grammar, and punctuation errors.

You may wish to draft and edit your essay on the computer.

Evaluation Criteria

Your teacher will be looking for:

1. **Statement of purpose**
   - Did you clearly state the main idea?
   - Did you support your main idea with details and evidence?

2. **Organization**
   - Are the sections of your essay organized in a way that makes sense?
   - Did you use connecting words to link your ideas?
   - Is there a clear conclusion that sums up your main idea?

3. **Elaboration of evidence**
   - Did you include only evidence that is relevant to the topic?
   - Is there enough evidence to support your main idea?

4. **Language and vocabulary**
   - Did you use a formal tone?
   - Did you explain any vocabulary that may be unfamiliar to your audience?

5. **Conventions**
   - Did you follow the rules of grammar usage as well as punctuation, capitalization, and spelling?

Courage Comes in All Sizes

Response to Literature

Step 1 — Analyze the Model

Evaluate a student model that describes the narrator of a short story.

Step 2 — Practice the Task

Write a response to literature explaining how a setting influences a character's actions.

Step 3 — Perform the Task

Write a response to literature explaining what makes a character "larger than life."

The main character in a novel or short story can drive the plot and keep the reader fascinated. If the character is extraordinary in some way, it is up to a great writer to make the character believable at the same time. There is always some way to relate to a great character, but even as the reader gets to know what the character is like, each page can bring new surprises.

Each of the selections in this unit features a strong character who is not brought down by trouble. Instead, these characters show admirable courage in unexpected ways.

IN THIS UNIT, you will evaluate a student's description of a homeless boy who lives in an airport. Then you will write a response to a girl's adventures in a storm at sea. Finally, you will read and respond to a story about an unusual girl who is "larger than life."

How can a character show courage?

© Houghton Mifflin Harcourt Publishing Company

You will read:

- **A Short Story**
  Fly Away Home

You will analyze:

- **A Student Model**
  Calm Courage

Source: Short Story

Ms. Chang's student, Pilar Pérez, analyzed the following story in an essay about its narrator, Andrew. As you read, make notes in the side columns. Underline information that you find helpful.

Notes

Fly Away Home

by Eve Bunting

My dad and I live in an airport. That's because we don't have a home and the airport is better than the streets. We are careful not to get caught.

Mr. Slocum and Mr. Vail were caught last night.

"Ten green bottles, hanging on the wall," they sang. They were as loud as two moose bellowing.

Dad said they broke the first rule of living here. Don't get noticed.

Dad and I try not to get noticed. We stay among
10 the crowds. We change airlines.

"Delta, TWA, Northwest, we love them all," Dad says.

He and I wear blue jeans and blue T-shirts and blue jackets. We each have a blue zippered bag with a change of blue clothes. Not to be noticed is to look like nobody at all.

Once we saw a woman pushing a metal cart full of stuff. She wore a long dirty coat and she lay down across a row of seats in front of Continental Gate 6. 20 The cart, the dirty coat, the lying down were all noticeable. Security moved her out real fast.

Discuss and Decide

Why does Dad have the rule that they must not be noticed?

Dad and I sleep sitting up. We use different airport areas.

"Where are we tonight?" I ask.

Dad checks his notebook. "Alaska Air," he says. "Over in the other terminal."

That's OK. We like to walk.

We know some of the airport regulars by name and by sight. There's Idaho Joe and Annie Frannie and Mars Man. But we don't sit together.

"Sitting together will get you noticed faster than anything," Dad says.

Everything in the airport is on the move— passengers, pilots, flight attendants, cleaners with their brooms. Jets roar in, close to the windows.

Other jets roar out. Luggage bounces down chutes, escalators glide up and down, disappearing under floors. Everyone's going somewhere except Dad and me. We stay.

Once a little brown bird got into the main terminal and couldn't get out. It fluttered in the high, hollow spaces. It threw itself at the glass, fell panting on the floor, flew to a tall, metal girder, and perched there, exhausted.

"Don't stop trying," I told it silently. "Don't! You can get out!"

For days the bird flew around, dragging one wing. And then it found the instant when a sliding door was open and slipped through. I watched it rise. Its wing seemed OK.

"Fly, bird," I whispered. "Fly away home!"

Though I couldn't hear it, I knew it was singing. Nothing made me as happy as that bird.

The airport's busy and noisy even at night. Dad and I sleep anyway. When it gets quiet, between two and four A.M., we wake up.

"Dead time," Dad says. "Almost no flights coming in or going out."

At dead time there aren't many people around, so 60 we're extra careful.

In the mornings Dad and I wash up in one of the bathrooms, and he shaves. The bathrooms are crowded, no matter how early. And that's the way we like it.

Discuss and Decide

Why does the narrator relate to the bird's situation?

Strangers talk to strangers.

"Where did you get in from?"

"Three hours our flight was delayed. Man! Am I bushed!"

Dad and I, we don't talk to anyone.

70   We buy doughnuts and milk for breakfast at one of the cafeterias, standing in line with our red trays. Sometimes Dad gets me a carton of juice.

On the weekends Dad takes the bus to work. He's a janitor in an office in the city. The bus fare's a dollar each way.

On those days Mrs. Medina looks out for me. The Medinas live in the airport, too—Grandma, Mrs. Medina, and Denny, who's my friend.

He and I collect rented luggage carts that people
80   have left outside and return them for fifty cents each. If the crowds are big and safe, we offer to carry bags.

"Get this one for you, lady? It looks heavy."

Or, "Can I call you a cab?" Denny's real good at calling cabs. That's because he's seven already.

Sometimes passengers don't tip. Then Denny whispers, "Stingy!" But he doesn't whisper too loud. The Medinas understand that it's dangerous to be noticed.

90   When Dad comes home from work, he buys hamburgers for us and the Medinas. That's to pay them for watching out for me. If Denny and I've had a good day, we treat for pie. But I've stopped doing that. I save my money in my shoe.

"Will we ever have our own apartment again?" I ask Dad. I'd like it to be the way it was, before Mom died.

Discuss and Decide

What do the narrator's actions while his father is away tell you about his character?

"Maybe we will," he says. "If I can find more work. If we can save some money." He rubs my
100 head. "It's nice right here, though, isn't it, Andrew? It's warm. It's safe. And the price is right."

But I know he's trying all the time to find us a place. He takes newspapers from the trash baskets and makes pencil circles around letters and numbers. Then he goes to the phones. When he comes back he looks sad. Sad and angry. I know he's been calling about an apartment. I know the rents are too high for us.

"I'm saving money, too," I tell him, and I lift one
110 foot and point to my shoe.

Dad smiles. "Atta boy!"

"If we get a place, you and your dad can come live with us," Denny says.

"And if *we* get a place, you and your mom and your grandma can come live with *us*," I say.

"Yeah!"

We shake on it. That's going to be so great!

After next summer, Dad says, I have to start school.

120 "How?" I ask.

"I don't know. But it's important. We'll work it out."

Denny's mom says he can wait for a while. But Dad says I can't wait.

Sometimes I watch people meeting people.

"We missed you."

"It's so good to be home."

Sometimes I get mad, and I want to run at them and push them and shout, "Why do *you* have homes when we don't? What makes *you* so special? That would get us noticed, all right.

Sometimes I just want to cry. I think Dad and I will be here forever.

Then I remember the bird. It took a while, but a door opened. And when the bird left, when it flew free, I know it was singing.

Close Read

Why does thinking of the bird give the narrator hope? Cite evidence from the text in your response.

Analyze a Student Model

Read Pilar's response to literature closely. The red side notes are the comments that her teacher, Ms. Chang, wrote.

Pilar Pérez

February 18

Calm Courage

This is an effective way to introduce your ideas.

Everybody knows what courage is. It's traveling to the North Pole on foot, or running into a burning house to save a baby. But courage has a quieter side, too. In *Fly Away Home*, a five-year-old boy living a bleak life stays strong and doesn't give up hope.

Andrew's mother has died, and his father can't find enough work to support himself and his son. They live in an airport, and have to be careful not to be noticed. They pretend to be travelers, and move from terminal to terminal every day. They sleep sitting up.

These details from the text let the reader understand Andrew's situation.

Even though Andrew can't act like most children his age, he stays calm most of the time. He makes a little money by helping real passengers with his friend Denny, who also lives at the airport. They both dream of having real homes, and promise that the first to get one will share it with the other. "That's going to be so great!" says Andrew, keeping the dream alive.

One day a small bird gets trapped in the airport. Andrew watches as it struggles to escape. He silently encourages the bird to keep trying, and after several days the bird manages to fly out of the building. Andrew identifies with the bird, and he is very happy for it when it escapes.

Yes. This is exactly why this event is important to Andrew. Good insight!

Being homeless in an airport where everyone else has a home and can afford to travel does make Andrew discouraged sometimes. He remarks, "Everyone's going somewhere except Dad and me." He looks at the passengers and wants to ask them "What makes *you* so special?"

These quotes tell me how Andrew feels.

Andrew doesn't like the life he has to lead, but he doesn't complain. Like the planes and like the trapped bird, he believes he too will be able to fly away.

Great ending Pilar!

Discuss and Decide

Why does Andrew relate the bird's struggle to his own situation?

Responding to Literature

Literary elements such as characters, settings, and events work together to make a story. After you read, you may be asked to explain how these elements shape a story and how they interact.

Are the story's **characters** believable? Do they talk and act in their own individual ways?

Can a reader picture the story's **setting**? Do the place and time add to the mood and impact events?

Are the story's **events** convincing results of interactions among the characters and the setting?

Writing a Response to Literature

• Capture your ideas in a strong opening statement.

• Quote from the text to support your ideas.

• Explain how story elements work together.

Look back through *Fly Away Home*. Find two events that affect the narrator. Describe the events and the narrator's responses below.

_____

_____

_____

_____

_____

How does a setting influence a character's actions?

You will read:

- **An Excerpt from a Novel**

  "The Girl in the Chicken-Coop" from Ozma of Oz

You will write:

- **A Response to Literature**

  How does a setting influence a character's actions?

AS YOU READ You will write a response to the excerpt "The Girl in the Chicken-Coop" from *Ozma of Oz*. As you read, underline information that may be useful to you when you write your essay.

The Girl in the Chicken-Coop

by L. Frank Baum

At the time the wind began to blow, a ship was sailing far out upon the waters. When the waves began to tumble and toss and to grow bigger and bigger the ship rolled up and down, and tipped sidewise—first one way and then the other—and was jostled around so roughly that even the sailor-men had to hold fast to the ropes and railings to keep themselves from being swept away by the wind or pitched headlong into the sea.

10   And the clouds were so thick in the sky that the sunlight couldn't get through them; so that the day grew dark as night, which added to the terrors of the storm.

The Captain of the ship was not afraid, because he had seen storms before, and had sailed his ship through them in safety; but he knew that his passengers would be in danger if they tried to stay on deck, so he put them all into the cabin and told them to stay there until after the storm was over,

20 and to keep brave hearts and not be scared, and all would be well with them.

Now, among these passengers was a little Kansas girl named Dorothy Gale, who was going with her Uncle Henry to Australia, to visit some relatives they had never before seen. Uncle Henry, you must know, was not very well, because he had been working so hard on his Kansas farm that his health had given way and left him weak and nervous. So he left Aunt Em at home to watch after the hired men and to
30 take care of the farm, while he traveled far away to Australia to visit his cousins and have a good rest.

Discuss and Decide

Which details create a frightening setting?

Dorothy was eager to go with him on this journey, and Uncle Henry thought she would be good company and help cheer him up; so he decided to take her along. The little girl was quite an experienced traveller, for she had once been carried

40 by a cyclone as far away from home as the marvelous Land of Oz, and she had met with a good many adventures in that strange country before she managed to get back to Kansas again. So she wasn't easily frightened, whatever happened, and when the wind began to howl and whistle, and the waves began to tumble and toss, our

50 little girl didn't mind the uproar the least bit.

"Of course we'll have to stay in the cabin," she said to Uncle Henry and the other passengers, "and keep as quiet as possible until the storm is over. For the Captain says if we go on deck we may be blown overboard."

No one wanted to risk such an accident as that, you may be sure; so all the passengers stayed huddled up in the dark cabin, listening to the shrieking of the storm and the creaking of the masts

© Houghton Mifflin Harcourt Publishing Company • Image Credits: © WELBURNSTUART/Shutterstock

1. Analyze   2. Practice   3. Perform

60 and rigging and trying to keep from bumping into one another when the ship tipped sidewise.

Dorothy had almost fallen asleep when she was aroused with a start to find that Uncle Henry was missing. She couldn't imagine where he had gone, and as he was not very strong she began to worry about him, and to fear he might have been careless enough to go on deck. In that case he would be in great danger unless he instantly came down again.

The fact was that Uncle Henry had gone to lie

70 down in his little sleeping-berth, but Dorothy did not know that. She only remembered that Aunt Em had cautioned her to take good care of her uncle, so at once she decided to go on deck and find him, in spite of the fact that the tempest was now worse than ever, and the ship was plunging in a really dreadful manner. Indeed, the little girl found it was as much as she could do to mount the stairs to

80 the deck, and as soon as she got there the wind struck her so fiercely that it almost tore away the skirts of her dress. Yet Dorothy felt a sort of joyous excitement in defying the storm, and while she held fast to the railing she peered around through the gloom and

Discuss and Decide

What can you tell about Dorothy from her actions during the storm?

thought she saw the dim form of a man clinging to a mast not far away from her. This might be her uncle, so she called as loudly as she could:

90 "Uncle Henry! Uncle Henry!"

But the wind screeched and howled so madly that she scarce heard her own voice, and the man certainly failed to hear her, for he did not move.

Dorothy decided she must go to him; so she made a dash forward, during a lull in the storm, to where a big square chicken-coop had been lashed to the deck with ropes. She reached this place in safety, but no sooner had she seized fast hold of the slats of the big box in which the chickens were kept 100 than the wind, as if enraged because the little girl dared to resist its power, suddenly redoubled its fury. With a scream like that of an angry giant it tore away the ropes that held the coop and lifted it high into the air, with Dorothy still clinging to the slats.

1. Analyze   2. Practice   3. Perform

Around and over it whirled, this way and that, and a few moments later the chicken-coop dropped far away into the sea, where the big waves caught it and slid it up-hill to a foaming crest and then down-hill into a deep valley, as if it were nothing more than a plaything to keep them amused.

Dorothy had a good ducking, you may be sure, but she didn't loose her presence of mind even for a second. She kept tight hold of the stout slats and as soon as she could get the water out of her eyes she saw that the wind had ripped the cover from the coop, and the poor chickens were fluttering away in every direction, being blown by the wind until they looked like feather dusters without handles. The bottom of the coop was made of thick boards, so Dorothy found she was clinging to a sort of raft,

Discuss and Decide

What does the writer suggest about the storm when he describes the coop as "nothing more than a plaything"?

with sides of slats, which readily bore up her weight. After coughing the water out of her throat and getting her breath again, she managed to climb over the slats and stand upon the firm wooden bottom of the coop, which supported her easily enough.

"Why, I've got a ship of my own!" she thought, more amused than frightened at her sudden change of condition; and then, as the coop climbed up to the top of a big wave, she looked eagerly around for 130 the ship from which she had been blown.

It was far, far away, by this time. Perhaps no one on board had yet missed her, or knew of her strange adventure. Down into a valley between the waves the coop swept her, and when she climbed another crest the ship looked like a toy boat, it was such a long way off. Soon it had entirely disappeared in

1. Analyze   2. Practice   3. Perform

the gloom, and then Dorothy gave a sigh of regret at parting with Uncle Henry and began to wonder what was going to happen to her next.

140   Just now she was tossing on the bosom of a big ocean, with nothing to keep her afloat but a miserable wooden hen-coop that had a plank bottom and slatted sides, through which the water constantly splashed and wetted her through to the skin! And there was nothing to eat when she became hungry—as she was sure to do before long—and no fresh water to drink and no dry clothes to put on.

"Well, I declare!" she exclaimed, with a laugh. "You're in a pretty fix, Dorothy Gale, I can tell you!
150   and I haven't the least idea how you're going to get out of it!"

Close Read

What situations in the story show that Dorothy is courageous? Cite evidence from the text in your response.

_____

_____

_____

_____

Respond to Questions

In Step 2, you have read an excerpt from *Ozma of Oz*.
Use your notes and refer to the source as you answer the
questions. Your answers to will help you write your essay.

1. Why does Dorothy worry that Uncle Henry is missing from the cabin?

    a. Dorothy is afraid of the dark.

    b. He is not very strong.

    c. Dorothy can't go exploring without Uncle Henry.

    d. He might have decided against the trip.

2. According to the text, why is Dorothy not easily frightened?

    a. She always thought of danger as her own plaything.

    b. She kept herself much too busy to be afraid.

    c. She learned from Uncle Henry that fear was not a
    useful emotion.

    d. She had once been carried by a cyclone to the
    Land of Oz.

3. What is the best meaning of *defying* in "Yet Dorothy felt a sort of joyous
excitement in defying the storm . . ."?

    a. going against

    b. accepting

    c. ignoring

    d. moving quickly

1. Analyze   2. Practice   3. Perform

④ Prose Constructed-Response How does the storm change the setting of the story? Cite text evidence in your response.

_____

_____

_____

_____

_____

⑤ Prose Constructed-Response What problems does Dorothy face after she floats away on the chicken-coop? Cite evidence from the text in your response.

_____

_____

_____

_____

⑥ Prose Constructed-Response How is Dorothy's behavior when she thinks Uncle Henry is missing similar to the way she behaves when she is floating on the chicken-coop? Cite text evidence in your response.

_____

_____

_____

_____

Planning and Prewriting

Before you draft your essay, complete some important planning steps.

Before you start writing, determine your main idea. Look for supporting details to include in your essay. Complete the chart below to help you think about the way the setting influences Dorothy's actions.

Assignment
Write a response to the narrative to answer the question: How does a setting influence a character's actions?

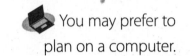 You may prefer to plan on a computer.

Examine Key Events

Event	Setting Details	What Dorothy Does
The Captain puts the passengers in the cabin.		
Dorothy realizes Uncle Henry is missing from the cabin.		
Dorothy sees a man on the ship's deck.		
Dorothy is in the chicken-coop.		

1. Analyze   2. Practice   3. Perform

Finalize Your Plan

You know what you want to say in your response to the excerpt. Now, it's time to plan the structure of your essay. You will save time and create a more organized, logical essay by planning the structure before you start writing.

Use your responses and notes from pp. 96–98 to complete the graphic organizer.

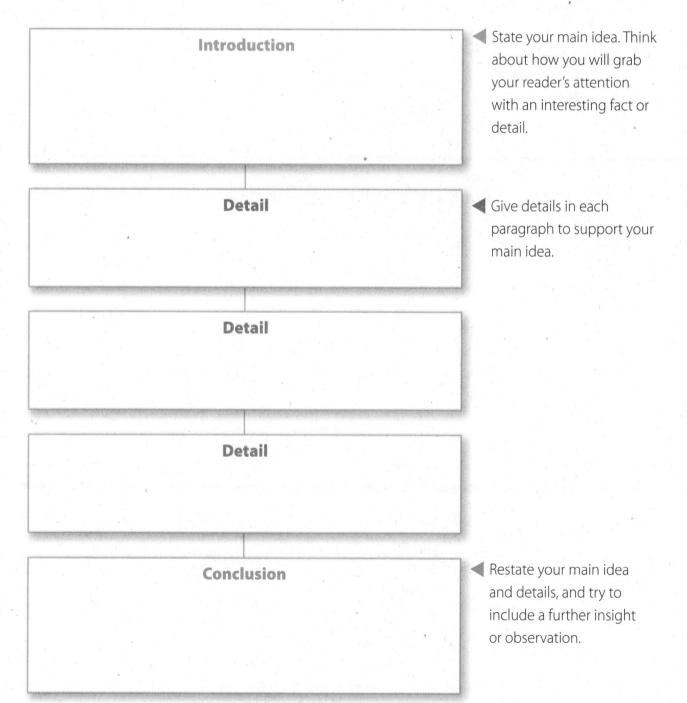

Introduction — State your main idea. Think about how you will grab your reader's attention with an interesting fact or detail.

Detail — Give details in each paragraph to support your main idea.

Detail

Detail

Conclusion — Restate your main idea and details, and try to include a further insight or observation.

Draft Your Essay

As you write, think about:

▶ **Purpose** *to analyze how setting influences a character's actions*

▶ **Clarity** *ideas that are straightforward and understandable*

▶ **Support** *examples from the sources that support your ideas*

▶ **Organization** *the logical structure for your essay*

▶ **Connecting Words** *words that link your ideas*

If you drafted your essay on the computer, you may wish to print it out.

Revision Checklist: Self-Evaluation

Use the checklist below to guide your self-evaluation.

Ask Yourself	Make It Better
1. Does the introduction grab the audience's attention and state your main idea?	A great introduction hooks your audience. Start with a question or a vivid image. Make sure you clearly state your main idea.
2. Do the details support your main idea?	In the body of your essay, give details that support your main idea.
3. Is your evidence accurate and relevant?	Make sure that you quote accurately from the text and that the evidence really relates to your point.
4. Does your essay flow well and connect the details to your main idea?	When you read what you have written, see if the sentences follow each other smoothly. Add connecting words to link the important ideas in your essay.
5. Does the last section restate your main idea?	In wrapping up your essay, restate your main idea and provide a summary of the details you gave to support your main idea.

Revision Checklist: Peer Review

Exchange your essay with a classmate, or read it out loud to your partner. As you read and comment on your partner's essay, focus on organization and evidence. Help your partner find parts of the draft that need to be revised.

What to Look For	Notes for My Partner
1. Does the introduction grab the audience's attention and state the main idea?	
2. Do the details support the main idea?	
3. Is the evidence accurate and relevant?	
4. Does the essay flow well and connect the details to the main idea?	
5. Does the last section restate the main idea?	

Support Your Ideas!

Review Your Use of Text Evidence

When you write a response to literature, the best way to support your ideas is to cite evidence from the literature itself. You can use quotes, give examples from the text, or tell what the characters say, think, or feel.

This paragraph was written about Dorothy's bravery in "The Girl in the Chicken-Coop." There is no direct evidence from the source material, but there is a lot of the writer's opinion.

> Dorothy is the bravest person on the ship. Dorothy is so brave, she doesn't even ask for help when she sees that Uncle Henry is missing from the cabin! Dorothy doesn't care that the chicken-coop floats away from the ship.

The paragraph can be improved by using quotes from the source to support the writer's idea.

> When Dorothy goes out into the storm, she does not feel afraid— she feels "a sort of joyous excitement." The chicken-coop separates from the ship, and she is "more amused than frightened." Dorothy views her problem as an adventure, and wonders "what was going to happen to her next."

Essay Tips

Cite from the Source

- State your ideas clearly, with no room for confusion.

- Support your ideas with evidence from the source material.

- Don't use unsupported opinions or assume that your audience already knows all the information that you know.

Edit

Edit your essay to correct spelling, grammar, and punctuation errors.

What makes a character "larger than life"?

You will read:

- **A Short Story**
  Lucy de Wilde

You will write:

- **A Response to Literature**
  What makes a character "larger than life"?

Lucy de Wilde

by Dina McClellan

"Boy and girls," says Ms. Haddad. "Today we'll be getting a new student in our class."

We look up, our Number 2 pencils idling like helicopters above our test booklets. Something exciting is about to happen. At Cedarcrest Falls Elementary, we're not used to excitement.

Cedarcrest Falls is where we live. Most of us kids were born here. Most of our parents were born here, too. We've known each other all our lives. A new student?

10   "She should be here soon, so I hope you'll all make her feel welcome," adds Ms. Haddad quickly, peering through the window in the classroom door.

There's a crackling from the loudspeaker. An announcement is on the way. We fall silent.

"Attention teachers, staff, and parent volunteers," says the voice of the assistant principal. "This is an alert!"

We're on the edge of our seats.

"We have a missing student.

20 New to Cedarcrest, a nine-year-old girl named Lucy. Please check your classrooms. Check all closets. Check the cafeteria. She may be carrying items from the meat locker."

The meat locker?

"I must go, boys and girls" says Ms. Haddad, grabbing her keys and sweater. "You may complete the rest of the test on your own. Just remember to press down hard when you fill in the ovals on the answer sheet." And she's gone.

30 A funny thing happens when a teacher leaves a classroom. Suddenly everything looks different. We glance from one to the other. We don't know what to do. And there's no one minding the store.

The class erupts. Soon we're standing on our desks throwing gerbil food at the Exit sign over the door.

Discuss and Decide

What details tell you that it is unusual to have a new student at Cedarcrest Falls Elementary?

Notes

Things go downhill from there.

Stella starts yelling that Billy stole her purse. Billy denies it, of course, but Billy denies everything, so Big Ralph takes the opportunity to knock him to the ground
40 where he can be conveniently walloped by several of the bigger boys, who are in turn pummeled by some of the even bigger girls.

The rest of us gather around, and although we have no idea what's happening we're having the best time. We're whooping it up, cheering them on, rooting for the good guy. Whoever that is.

Then, from out in the hallway comes a long, high, mournful wail. It sounds very much like a howl. Actually, it is a howl.

50 The door opens and in comes a stringy little girl, just bones and muscle. We all gawp at her, even though we've been taught not to gawp. Her hair, super-scraggly and long enough to sit on, is pure white underneath, black on top. She slinks rather than walks. Her eyes are so ice-blue they make you shiver.

© Houghton Mifflin Harcourt Publishing Company • Image Credits: © JUPITERIMAGES/BananaStock/Alamy

We stare at the floor so as not to meet them. Suddenly, we're ashamed of our bad behavior. All of us. Even if we weren't fighting.

60 We make a path for her, and she walks through like it's her right.

"Sorry I'm late," the girl says, "but I felt like being somewhere else. Hey—can someone open a window in here?"

We tell her the windows don't open.

"Don't open?" she cries. "That's probably why you're all fighting!"

"Billy stole my lunch money!" Stella blurts out.

"Stole your lunch money, eh?" The girl paces around, sniffing. Then she stops and focuses on something. It's
70 Stella's backpack. The girl circles around it three times clockwise and then plunks herself down on the floor.

While we all watch open-mouthed, she zips open the backpack, digs around for a second, and then pulls out a little change purse in the shape of a heart. She jiggles the coins. They sound like sleigh bells.

"It was in my backpack the whole time!," says Stella. "I'm sorry, Billy! "

And then everyone is apologizing to Billy. Even Big Ralph, who never apologizes to anyone.

80 "How did you know about Stella's coins?" someone asks.

Discuss and Decide

What do the children find strange about the new student?

She shrugs. "Smelled them, of course. They smell just like metal and Stella tucked behind a backpack and inside a purse. Where I come from, you sometimes have to look for food beneath the snow . . ."

"Where *do* you come from? Who *are* you?" someone finally asks.

"My name is Lucy de Wilde," the girl says, with a flash of white teeth. "That's my clan name, actually. The name I was given by the wolves after they kidnapped me and brought me up as one of their own."

It doesn't get better than this.

"Oh, I'm still human," she's quick to point out. "But I have some . . . wolfish traits I can't seem to shake. Blame it on the way I was brought up. Or you could credit it to the way I was brought up."

"Tell us," pleads Stella, "what traits?"

"Well, let's see. I hate being told what to do," she says, scrutinizing Stella and waving her hand. We notice that her nails are long and sharp. "And," she continues, "I'm hungry all the time—which reminds me, I'm starving. Why don't we all go down to the cafeteria and have some—" she sniffs the air, "—even I don't know what that is."

No one moves.

"What's the matter?" she says. "Aren't you hungry?"

We *are* hungry, we tell her. *Very* hungry. But it's not lunchtime yet. We have to wait until the bell rings, at 12:45.

"Why?" she asks.

We explain that it's just the rules. Besides, we have to wait for Ms. Haddad.

"Why?" she asks again.

"Because she's our teacher and we have to stay together."

"Oh," she says with a disappointed sigh. "You have your rules, I have mine."

She wanders over to the locked window, which looks out onto busy Cedarcrest Street, and watches the cars go by. Then she freezes and fixes her gaze on something. We all get curious and troop over to the window.

We see what she's been looking at. It's a kitten! The little thing is trying to cross the street, darting from car to car as traffic whizzes by!

120

Close Read

What are Lucy's "wolfish traits"? Cite text evidence in your response.

Lucy de Wilde's eyes get cold and hard. She slowly gulps in a gigantic breath through her clenched teeth. We realize then that the kitten's biggest problem won't come from the cars. It will come from Lucy de Wilde.

130   Suddenly, and without warning, the girl hurls herself against the window, smashing it to bits, and leaps out into the street. She tears off in the direction of the kitten.

Nooooooo!

We're about to witness an act of wolfish violence. Some of us scream, and most of us close our eyes. From the street comes a long, lonely *Awoooooooooo!*

"Look!" Big Ralph says then.

We look, and this is what we see: Lucy de Wilde with the kitten in her arms, nuzzling its face, and a woman

140   in a jogging suit, carrying a bag of groceries, running toward them. It's clear that the kitten belongs to her.

We watch as the woman, tears of joy running down her face, gives Lucy de Wilde a great big hug.

"*Awwwwwwwww*," we say. So Lucy de Wilde is a human after all!

We're about to go back to our seats when we see Lucy de Wilde snatch the woman's groceries right out of

150   her hands and lope off toward the woods.

Respond to Questions

These questions will help you think about the source you've read. Use your notes and refer to the source to answer the questions. Your answers to these questions will help you write your essay.

1. Why does Ms. Haddad leave the classroom?
   a. She has to prepare lunch in the cafeteria.
   b. She has to join the search for Lucy.
   c. The children have to complete the test alone.
   d. She goes to look for Stella's lunch money.

2. Why does Lucy think the children are fighting?
   a. The classroom windows don't open.
   b. The children are very hungry.
   c. There is no teacher there to stop them.
   d. Stella and Billy always argue and fight.

3. What does Lucy do with the kitten in the street?
   a. She chases it toward the woods.
   b. She returns it to its owner.
   c. She keeps it for her own.
   d. She gives it to a stranger.

4. Which statement tells you the schoolchildren are interested in Lucy?
   a. "An announcement is on the way."
   b. "We glance from one to the other."
   c. "It doesn't get better than this."
   d. "We see what she's been looking at."

5 **Prose Constructed-Response** How do the children react when they first meet Lucy? Cite text evidence in your response.

_____

_____

_____

_____

6 **Prose Constructed-Response** Why are the children surprised by what happens with Lucy and the kitten? Cite text evidence in your response.

_____

_____

_____

_____

7 **Prose Constructed-Response** In what way does Lucy's behavior reflect her statement that "You have your rules, I have mine"?

_____

_____

_____

_____

Write the Essay

Read the assignment.

Assignment
Write a response to literature that answers the question: What makes a character "larger than life"?

Plan

Use the graphic organizer to help you outline the structure of your response to literature.

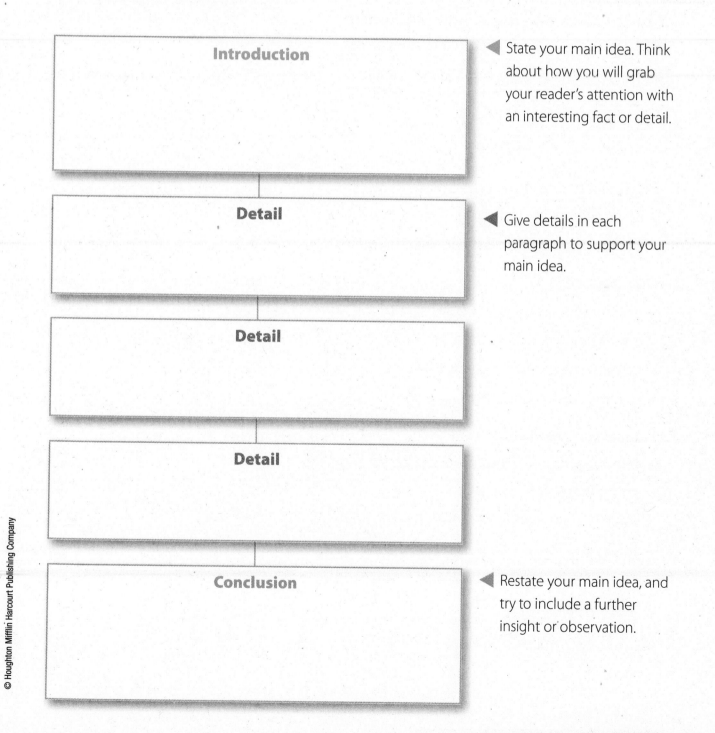

Introduction

◀ State your main idea. Think about how you will grab your reader's attention with an interesting fact or detail.

Detail

◀ Give details in each paragraph to support your main idea.

Detail

Detail

Conclusion

◀ Restate your main idea, and try to include a further insight or observation.

Draft

Use your notes and completed graphic organizer to write a first draft of your opinion essay.

Revise and Edit

Look back over your essay and compare it to the Evaluation Criteria. Revise your essay and edit it to correct spelling, grammar, and punctuation errors.

You may wish to draft and edit your essay on the computer.

Evaluation Criteria

Your teacher will be looking for:

1. **Statement of purpose**
   - Is your main idea stated clearly?
   - Did you support your main idea with details?

2. **Organization**
   - Are the sections of your essay organized in a way that makes sense?
   - Is there a smooth flow from beginning to end?
   - Did you use connecting words?
   - Is there a clear conclusion?

3. **Elaboration of evidence**
   - Did you accurately quote words from the text that support your main idea?
   - Did you include only evidence that is relevant to the topic?

4. **Conventions**
   - Did you use proper punctuation, capitalization, and spelling?

Wrong Place, Wrong Time

Narrative

Step 1
Analyze the Model

Evaluate a narrative about what happens to a lone flamingo among hundreds of swans.

Step 2
Practice the Task

Write a narrative about what happens when a train schedule and an audition schedule get mixed up.

Step 3
Perform the Task

Write a narrative about what happens when you go back in time to ancient Rome.

Writers tell a series of events in a narrative. Whether it is factual or made-up, a good narrative is always believable. For example, a made-up narrative about a famous historical person will ring true when some details about that person are accurate. Although the story itself isn't factual, it is believable because it includes details that are real.

Fictional narratives don't just come from a writer's imagination. Many writers find inspiration from informational texts such as newspaper articles, encyclopedia entries, or online reports. They read sources and use the information in them to support the story they want to tell.

You will want to base your own narratives on sources that you've read. You will feel more comfortable writing about your subject and create a more engaging story for your reader.

IN THIS UNIT, you will evaluate a story about what happens when a huge crowd finds it includes a single outsider. Then you will read two informational sources and write a story about what happens when you misread the schedules for an important event. Finally, you will read two sources and write a story about what happens when you show up thousands of years in the past.

What happens to a lone flamingo among swans?

You will read:

- **A Travel Article**
  Abbotsbury Swannery

- **An Informational Article**
  The Flamingo

You will analyze:

- **A Student Model**
  Who's the Ugly Duckling?

Source 1: Travel Article

Ms. Parker's student, Tanya Wright, read the following text as a source for her narrative about a flamingo that lives among swans. As you read, make notes in the side columns and underline useful information.

Notes

by Marcel Smith

The small village of Abbotsbury lies on the south coast of England. It is home to the world's only supervised colony of mute swans. This swannery has been there since the year 1393. Each year, hundreds of swan pairs hatch and raise their cygnets (baby swans). The male swan guards as the female nurses the eggs. Swans stay with their partners for their whole lives.

Mute swans do not honk like other swans. However, they do hiss and make snoring sounds and grunts.

They are the largest water birds, weighing as much as 50 pounds, and are the heaviest flying bird. (Ostriches and emus cannot fly.) Swans are also the fastest water birds, both swimming and flying.

Swans feed on plants that grow in shallow water. They reach down into the water with their long necks, but they don't dive. At Abbotsbury, the swans live in a natural lagoon formed by a long beach that is separated from the mainland.

The Abbotsbury Swannery is not a zoo, even though people visit to watch and feed the birds. The swans are free to fly away whenever they want to. They do help pay for their keep, though. They provide feathers for the helmets of the Queen's bodyguard.

Notes

Source 2: Informational Article

For years a lone flamingo lived among the swans in Abbotsbury Swannery. This article was the second source Tanya read for her narrative. Continue to make notes in the side columns and underline information as you read.

Notes

The Flamingo

by Jenny Madrid

There's a cave painting in Spain from 7,000 years ago that shows a bird that is unmistakably a flamingo. Flamingos have always attracted attention! They have a distinctive pink or orange color, and can be five feet tall. The color is a result of their diet of small organisms. (Carrots and beets would make people orange too, if they ate enough of them.) Flamingos eat by sucking up mud and water from the bottom as they wade. They filter the mud and water through their beaks to obtain food.

Flamingos usually live around saltwater inlets or lakes, in groups that range in size from several pairs up to many thousands of birds. Having other birds around is protection for a flamingo when it is eating with its head in the mud.

Flamingos can growl, babble, and honk. They are noted for the habit of standing on one leg. Nobody knows for sure why they do this. It might just be comfortable for them.

Close Read

In what ways are swans and flamingos similar? In what ways do they differ? Cite evidence from the text in your response.

Notes

Analyze a Student Model

After the class read the sources, Ms. Parker asked her students to write a narrative about a lone flamingo living among a group of swans. Tanya wrote a story about how the flamingo and the swans got along. Read Tanya's narrative closely. The red notes are the comments that Ms. Parker wrote.

Tanya Wright

March 8

Who's the Ugly Duckling?

"Splish, splash" is a good phrase to use here. It captures the reader's imagination and explains the setting.

Splish, splash! Splish, splash! The flamingo waded through the water, occasionally dipping his head to the bottom to feed.

"Would you look at that!" hissed a swan. "What on earth is it wearing? And what's with those legs?" Her friends grunted and snorted. There were hundreds of them. They stretched their necks and peered past each other to get a better look at the strange pink intruder.

The flamingo stood balanced on one leg. He gazed calmly across the dense crowd of swans. Then he honked, "Is there bleach in this water?"

The swans darted perplexed looks at one another. "Bleach?" they muttered. "Bleach in this water? What? There's nothing in this water. It's wonderful. It keeps us bright and snowy. There's no . . . Oh."

The flamingo was pleased with his joke and honked with laughter so hard that he toppled over. And that made the swans grunt and flap their wings with delight.

When the merriment had died down, a swan leaned over to the flamingo. "I like your neck," he said.

"I like your neck, too," replied the flamingo.

Your dialogue reveals a lot about the characters.

The facts you used really push your story along, Tanya.

Discuss and Decide

What facts from the sources did Tanya use in her narrative?

Set the Scene!

The setting is the time and place of the action in a story. A good writer will include memorable images and concrete details to make the setting come alive. In her story, Tanya could have described the setting more realistically so the reader could better picture where the action takes place.

Here is a part of Tanya's story:

> The flamingo was pleased with his joke and honked with laughter so hard that he toppled over.

How could Tanya describe the scene better? She could add a sentence that lets the reader "see" the setting. Here's an example:

> The calm water erupted in a splash, sending out rings of ripples around the flamingo's upturned leg.

Story Tips

Remember These Tips!

- Imagine the setting in your mind. Then, try to put it down in words. Do your words accurately describe what you are thinking of?

- Imagine that a reader will draw a picture based on your words. Would it look like the setting you are writing about?

Look back through Tanya's story. Find one description of the setting that you could improve. Rewrite the description and exchange your work with a partner. Ask your partner if your writing lets him or her better imagine the setting.

What happens when two schedules get mixed up?

You will read:

- **A Train Schedule**
  Timetable for North Line: Main St.–Central Station

- **An Audition Flyer**
  Talent Search America

You will write:

- **A Narrative**
  What happens when two schedules get mixed up?

Source 1: Train Schedule

AS YOU READ You will write a narrative about what happens when two schedules get mixed up. As you read, underline information that may be useful to you when you write your story.

Timetable for North Line
Main St. – Central Station

This schedule is for use by riders who live near the Main St. stop.

North Line: Main St. – Central Station					
Departing From:	**Train #**				
	1	**2**	**3**	**4**	**5**
Main St. (Your Stop)	7:00 A.M.	9:00 A.M.	11:00 A.M.	1:00 P.M.	3:00 P.M.
Park Plaza	8:30 A.M.	10:30 A.M.	12:30 P.M.	2:30 P.M.	4:30 P.M.
Beacon Arena	9:00 A.M.	11:00 A.M.	1:00 P.M.	3:00 P.M.	5:00 P.M.
Roosevelt Ave.	9:30 A.M.	11:30 A.M.	1:30 P.M.	3:30 P.M.	5:30 P.M.
Central Station	10:00 A.M.	12:00 P.M.	2:00 P.M.	4:00 P.M.	6:00 P.M.

1. Analyze   **2. Practice**   3. Perform

Source 2: Audition Flyer

Talent Search America

Talent Search America is looking for stars right in your town! Come on down to Beacon Arena this Friday and show our celebrity judges what you've got! Check the schedule below to find out when and where your event is.

Event	Audition Time	Description
Gymnastics/ Acrobatics	9:00 A.M.	Calling all tumblers, trampoline jumpers and trapeze artists, all handstanders and high-wire walkers! Competitors will have 5 minutes to perform a routine for our judges. All equipment (bars, nets, wires, ropes, etc.) will be provided.
Dance	11:00 A.M.	All styles are welcome, so bring your tango, ballet, square dancing, hip-hop, and waltzes. Both solo dancers and groups will have 3 minutes to perform a routine. Performances will be judged on technique, style, and uniqueness.
Singing	1:00 P.M.	All genres are welcome, from pop to R&B to opera. Both solo singers and groups will have 3 minutes to perform. Performances will be judged on technique and uniqueness.
Bands	3:00 P.M.	Each band must have at least 3 members. As with singing, all genres are welcome, so whether you're rock, jazz, country, or even classical, come on down! All performers must bring their own instruments. Performers will be judged on technique, songwriting, and uniqueness.
Other	5:00 P.M.	Have a talent that doesn't fit into the categories above? Show us here. All competitors will have 5 minutes to perform and will be judged on technique and entertainment value.

Discuss and Decide

What might cause a dancer to accidentally show up at the singing audition?

Respond to Questions

In Step 2, you have looked at a train schedule and an
audition flyer. Use your notes and refer to the sources
as you answer the questions. Your answers will help you
write your narrative.

1 Which of the following adds to your understanding about the bands
audition?

   a. "Have a talent that doesn't fit into the categories above?
   Show us here."

   b. "Performances will be judged on technique, style, and
   uniqueness."

   c. "All performers must bring their own instruments."

   d. "Both solo singers and groups will have 3 minutes to perform."

2 Which train would someone take to get to the dance audition on time?

   a. 10:00 A.M. from Central Station

   b. 10:30 A.M. from Park Plaza

   c. 11:00 A.M. from Main St.

   d. 1:00 P.M. from Beacon Arena

3 What information is explained in Source 1 but not in Source 2?

   a. a schedule of events for Talent Search America

   b. what time the singing audition starts

   c. how long it takes to get to Beacon Arena

   d. where the talent search is taking place

1. Analyze   2. Practice   3. Perform

4 **Prose Constructed-Response** What would happen if you took the 3:00 P.M. train from Main St. to go to the band audition? Cite text evidence in your response.

_____

_____

_____

_____

5 **Prose Constructed-Response** What information in Source 2 is most useful for understanding the way events are judged? Cite text evidence in your response.

_____

_____

_____

_____

_____

6 **Prose Constructed-Response** Explain why someone would need information from both Source 1 and Source 2 to go to the talent search. Cite text evidence in your response.

_____

_____

_____

_____

Planning and Prewriting

Before you draft your narrative, complete some important planning steps.

Collect Information

Before you start writing, think about the sources you've read. Look for interesting facts and details that you can include in your narrative. Complete the chart below with information from each source.

Assignment

You live on Main St. and want to go to the Talent Search America auditions. However, you mix up the times written on the train schedule and the audition flyer. Write a narrative about what happens.

 You may prefer to plan on a computer.

Source	Interesting Facts to Use in My Narrative
Train Schedule Timetable for North Line: Main St.–Central Station	
Audition Flyer Talent Search America	

Finalize Your Plan

You know what you want to include in your narrative. Now, it's time to plan the structure of your story. You will save time and create a more organized, logical narrative by planning the structure before you start writing.

Use your responses and notes from pp. 128–130 to complete the graphic organizer.

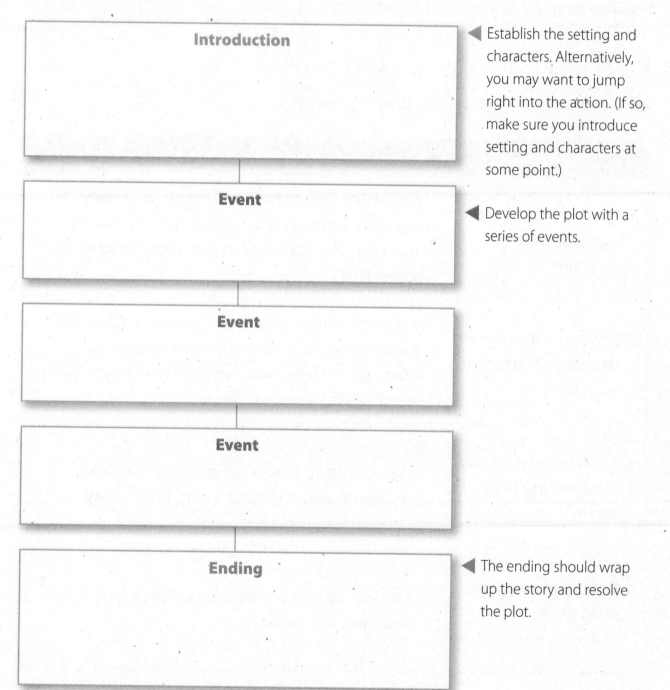

Introduction

◀ Establish the setting and characters. Alternatively, you may want to jump right into the action. (If so, make sure you introduce setting and characters at some point.)

Event

◀ Develop the plot with a series of events.

Event

Event

Ending

◀ The ending should wrap up the story and resolve the plot.

Draft Your Narrative

As you write, think about:

▶ **Purpose** *to entertain or engage the reader*

▶ **Clarity** *straightforward, understandable ideas and descriptions*

▶ **Support** *factual details that help make your story believable*

▶ **Organization** *the logical structure for your story*

▶ **Connecting Words** *words that link your ideas*

Revision Checklist: Self-Evaluation

Use the checklist below to guide your self-evaluation.

Ask Yourself	Make It Better
1. Does the introduction grab your audience's attention?	A great introduction hooks your audience. Clearly introduce the characters and setting. Or, jump right into the action. (Make sure to introduce characters and setting later.)
2. Do you use dialogue and description to develop your story?	Include descriptive details to help readers picture the characters and setting. Use dialogue to reveal how characters feel or how they respond to situations. Make sure the dialogue sounds natural.
3. Are events in your story presented in a clear order?	Make sure that the sequence of events is clear. Add transitional words to link the events in your story.
4. Does your conclusion bring all the action to an end?	Make sure that the ending resolves the plot, and seems natural and not rushed.

Revision Checklist: Peer Review

Exchange your story with a classmate, or read it out loud to your partner. As you read and comment on your partner's story, focus on the elements of a good narrative. Help your partner find parts of the draft that need to be revised.

What to Look For	Notes for My Partner
1. Does the introduction grab the audience's attention?	
2. Do dialogue and description develop the story?	
3. Are events in the story presented in a clear order?	
4. Does the conclusion bring all the action to an end?	

Writing Dialogue

Dialogue is conversation between two or more characters in a story. It can be used to reveal the characters' personalities, explain situations, and move events along. It can also be used to reveal important details about those situations and events.

This example of dialogue explains a situation:

> "Is this the band rehearsal?" Dwayne asked as he pulled out his violin.
>
> "Uh, if you didn't notice, we're rehearsing for a play right now," a girl wearing a crown told him.
>
> "Those guys look like musicians!" Dwayne joked as two pirates ran by him.
>
> "Hey," the girl said. "We need a jester for scene 2. Want to try out?"

Story Tips

Remember These Tips When Writing Dialogue

- Words that characters say appear in quotation marks. Make sure that it's clear who is speaking.

- One character may not know everything that another character knows. Be sure your dialogue reflects the characters' knowledge of events in the story.

- Make sure the dialogue adds something to the story. It might reveal how characters feel or explain the action.

Edit

Edit your essay to correct spelling, grammar, and punctuation errors.

What would happen if you went back in time?

You will read:

- **An Informational Article**
  Life in Ancient Rome

- **A List**
  What to Pack for My Trip to Rome!

You will write:

- **A Narrative**
  What would happen if you went back in time?

LIFE IN ANCIENT ROME

by Dmitri Moskal

Rome was the capital of Italy, and life there could be good—if you were wealthy. Your home would be a house with many beautifully decorated rooms surrounding courtyards and gardens. Your servants and those you held as slaves would do your bidding.

If you were not wealthy, you would live in an apartment building. The higher the floor, the smaller the apartment, and the lower the rent you would pay. There would be more stairs and perhaps no heat or
10   water. There was also less chance of escaping a fire.

Some parts of everyday life were the same for rich and poor. The person in charge of a household was always a man. Whatever duties there were in the home, the man would control them. After work each day, people from all classes would go to the public baths to bathe, exercise, and chat. All Romans also followed the same traditions for the evening meal, though they didn't eat the same food. Rich families ate eggs, shellfish, or vegetables, followed by meat
20   and vegetables, then fruit or pastry. Most Romans, however, ate only bread and porridge.

Slavery was common. People held as slaves were prisoners of war or those purchased from beyond Roman lands. They were the property of their rich owners, and could be sold, rented, or even killed at any time. However, Romans often freed their slaves.

Enslaved people worked everywhere and looked like any other Romans. The government thought of making them wear special clothing for identification.
30 They dropped the plan once they realized it would also let enslaved people identify each other, and see that they were numerous enough to rise up in revolt.

The poor were also numerous. The rich occupied them with "bread and circuses." People were given free wheat and were provided free entertainments such as chariot races and gladiator fights. As many as 12 chariots competed at a time, and drivers might be thrown from their chariots and trampled to death by the other horses. Gladiator fights, by their nature,
40 were dangerous. They were fights to the death! Successful gladiators could get very wealthy. This possibility attracted free men to the sport, as well as those who could not refuse.

Rome was a city of contrasts. It was home to emperors and to people held as slaves. It was the center of the world.

Close Read

What were two differences between the lives of rich and poor people in ancient Rome? Cite text evidence in your response.

What to Pack for My Trip to Rome!

✔ documents
✔ cash
✔ glasses
✔ watch
✔ camera
✔ laptop
✔ smartphone
✔ books
✔ pen
✔ notebook
✔ hairbrush
✔ shampoo
✔ toothbrush and toothpaste
✔ clothes and shoes
✔ umbrella

Discuss and Decide

Which items on the list would most surprise people from the past?

1. Analyze   2. Practice   **3. Perform**

Respond to Questions

These questions will help you think about the sources you've read. Use your notes and refer to the sources to answer the questions. Your answers to these questions will help you write your story.

1 What did most Romans eat at dinner?

    a. meat and vegetables

    b. bread and porridge

    c. a shellfish or eggs

    d. vegetables

2 Why did the Roman government give up the idea of having enslaved people wear special clothing?

    a. The clothing would make it hard for the enslaved people to work.

    b. Enslaved people would see that they were numerous enough to revolt.

    c. The rents in the higher apartments would get more expensive.

    d. People would not know who owned the enslaved people.

3 Which statement explains the way the wealthy controlled most Romans?

    a. "The person in charge of a household was always a man."

    b. "All Romans also followed the same traditions . . ."

    c. "Enslaved people worked everywhere and looked like any other Romans."

    d. "People were given free wheat and were provided free entertainments . . ."

④ Which items on the list would surprise ancient Romans the least?

   a. smartphone

   b. camera

   c. watch

   d. clothes and shoes

⑤ **Prose Constructed-Response** In what ways were rich and poor Romans alike? Cite text evidence in your response.

_____

_____

_____

_____

⑥ **Prose Constructed-Response** Which source would be most helpful for planning a vacation? Cite text evidence in your response.

_____

_____

_____

_____

⑦ **Prose Constructed-Response** Explain whether or not a laptop and smartphone would be useful in ancient Rome.

_____

_____

_____

_____

Write the Narrative

Read the assignment.

Assignment
You set out for a vacation to Rome, and you reach the city safely. The only thing is, you arrive there 2,000 years ago! Write a narrative about your vacation.

Plan

Use the graphic organizer to help you outline the structure of your narrative.

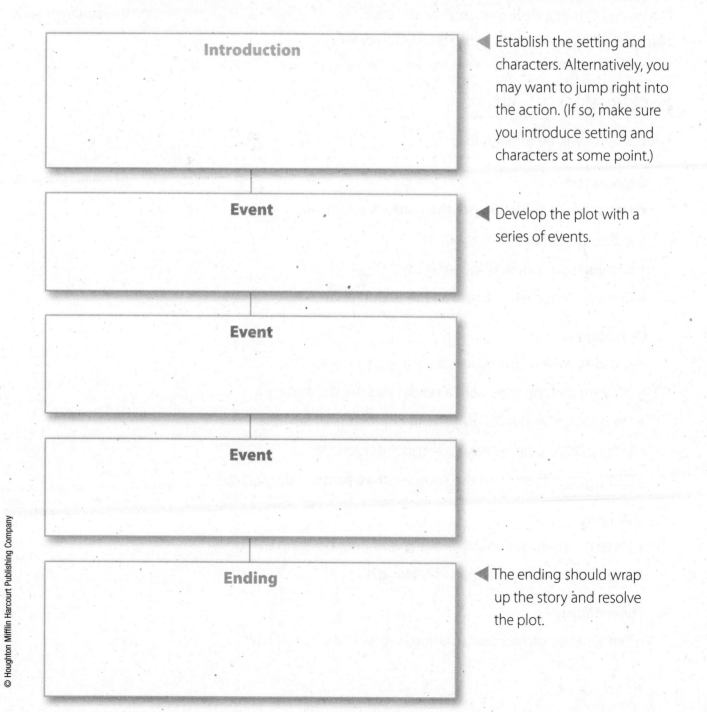

Introduction

◀ Establish the setting and characters. Alternatively, you may want to jump right into the action. (If so, make sure you introduce setting and characters at some point.)

Event

◀ Develop the plot with a series of events.

Event

Event

Ending

◀ The ending should wrap up the story and resolve the plot.

Draft

Use your notes and completed graphic organizer to write a first draft of your narrative.

Revise and Edit

Look back over your story and compare it to the Evaluation Criteria. Revise your story and edit it to correct spelling, grammar, and punctuation errors.

You may wish to draft and edit your story on the computer.

Evaluation Criteria

Your teacher will be looking for:

1. **Organization**
    - Does the introduction get the reader's attention?
    - Is the sequence of events clear?
    - Did you use connecting words?
    - Does the conclusion bring all the action to an end?

2. **Descriptions**
    - Is it clear where and when the story takes place?
    - Do your descriptions help a reader picture the setting?
    - Do descriptive details make your characters believable?
    - Does each character have a distinct personality?
    - Did you use facts from the sources to make the story realistic?

3. **Dialogue**
    - Does the dialogue sound realistic and help develop the story?
    - Is it clear which character is speaking?

4. **Conventions**
    - Did you use proper punctuation, capitalization, and spelling?

On Your Own

Mixed Practice

Task 1

Research Simulation

Opinion Essay

Should people send handwritten letters today?

Task 2

Research Simulation

Informative Essay

How have people used Morse code to communicate?

Task 3

Response to Literature

How does Amos's point of view affect his description of Ben Franklin?

Task 4

Research Simulation

Narrative

What is life like when the electrical grid is shut down?

Research Simulation

Opinion Essay

Your Assignment

You will read two sources on handwritten letters. Then you will write an opinion essay about whether people should send handwritten letters today.

Time Management: Opinion Essay Task

There are two parts to most formal writing tests. Both parts of the tests are timed, so it's important to use your limited time wisely.

Part 1: Read Sources

(35)

Preview the Assignment

35 minutes

You will have 35 minutes to read two texts about whether people should send handwritten letters today. You will then answer questions about the sources.

How Many?

How many pages of reading? [ ]

How many multiple-choice questions? [ ]

How many prose constructed-response questions? [ ]

How do you plan to use the 35 minutes?

Estimated time to read:

"Handwritten Letters Are Important" [ ] minutes

"Handwritten Letters Belong in the Past" [ ] minutes

Estimated time to answer questions? [ ] minutes

Total   **35 minutes**

---

35 minutes! That's not much time.

Preview the questions. This will help you know which information you'll need to find as you read.

Underline and take notes as you read. You probably won't have time to reread.

This is a lot to do in a short time.

© Houghton Mifflin Harcourt Publishing Company

Part 2: Write the Essay

Plan and Write an Opinion Essay

85 minutes

You will have 85 minutes to plan, write, revise, and edit your essay.

Your Plan

Before you start to write, decide on your opinion. Then think about the reasons and evidence you will use to support your opinion.

How do you plan to use the 85 minutes?

Estimated time for planning the essay?	_____ minutes
Estimated time for writing?	_____ minutes
Estimated time for editing?	_____ minutes
Estimated time for checking spelling, grammar, and punctuation?	_____ minutes
Total	**85** minutes

How much time do you have? Pay attention to the clock!

Be sure to leave enough time for this step!

Reread your essay, making sure that the points are clear. Check that there are no spelling or punctuation mistakes.

Your Assignment

You will read two texts and then write an opinion essay about whether people should send handwritten letters today.

Complete the following steps as you plan and compose your essay.

1. Read an editorial about why handwritten letters are important.

2. Read an editorial about why handwritten letters are not important.

3. Answer questions about the sources.

4. Plan, write, and revise your essay.

Part 1 (35 minutes)

You will now read the sources. Take notes on important facts and details as you read. You can refer to the sources and your notes as you write your essay.

Handwritten Letters Are Important

By Lucida Bright

There's something missing in this digital age of communicating through laptops, tablets, and smartphones. Letters may not be handwritten very often today, but they still have an impact on anyone who receives them.

It takes no time at all to "like" a status, or text someone a quick message, but a handwritten letter takes time. Writing by hand is slower than typing, so when you receive a handwritten note or letter, you know the person took time to think about you. An emailed thank you note, for instance, gets to the point quickly. But a handwritten thank you note shows that the person writing it appreciated your time and effort, and is giving time and effort in return. Your brain also has to work more when you write by hand, because there isn't a spell-check for handwritten letters.

Many people will hold on to handwritten letters they receive. They might keep the letters out on display, or put them away in a memory box. The letters can remind them of the person who wrote the letter. Once an email has been read, many people will delete it. People save handwritten mail because it is more personal.

A letter can even make you feel close to someone who is far away. Email is nice, but you probably wouldn't put it out on display for everyone to see. Emails aren't fun to look at!

You can touch and feel a letter. A letter is touched
30 by both the writer and the person receiving the letter, which is another way that letters make people feel close to one another.

Letters also feel more private. You can post a message on a site for everyone to see, but when you write a letter to someone, the only person you have written your message for is the person receiving the note. You may be able to express yourself more honestly when you are writing to one person.

If you have received a letter from someone, you
40 know that it is a great feeling. It may be easier to write an email, but sending someone a handwritten letter will always be the best way to show people that you are thinking about them. And getting a letter from a friend sure beats the junk mail and bills we often find in our mailboxes!

Am I on Track?

Actual Time Spent Reading

Handwritten Letters Belong in the Past

By Gill Sans

Handwritten letters are no longer necessary in this world of digital technology. In the past, handwritten letters were the fastest way for people to communicate information to people far away. Then the telegraph came along, then computers, and then the Internet. Now, handwritten letters are outdated.

Students today take exams online. College students bring tablets to class instead of notebooks. It's quicker to type something than it is to write

10 it. When you need to tell something to someone immediately, an email or text message is the best way to send the information.

Handwritten letters or notes can be hard to read, because every person's handwriting is different. Some people's writing is just about impossible to read. Typing on an electronic device means that what you write will be easily read by others—and yourself!

If you write something by hand, you might lose

20 it. A letter could get lost or damaged in the mail. When you send a message electronically, you know that it will be delivered. If you throw a letter away, it is gone forever, but sometimes you can recover

a deleted email, or ask the person who sent the message to send it again.

The information you type into a computer can be saved in multiple places. If you email a document to someone, you will have a copy on your computer, and the other person will have a copy on 30 his computer. You can even access a document on another device, such as a smartphone or tablet. This is a good way for students to share notes from class, or work together on a school project.

It's easier to make changes when you are writing something electronically. You can fix mistakes easily and edit sentences to say what you mean. You can see what it looks like, and make up your mind. If you didn't fix the sentences enough, you can even change it again. You can't do that with pencil and 40 paper!

Technology is meant to make our lives easier. We have the technology at our fingertips. Why should we go back to doing things the way we did them in the past, when we can do them better and more quickly?

Am I on Track?

Actual Time Spent Reading

Questions

Answer the following questions. You may refer to your reading notes, and you should cite text evidence in your responses. Your answers to these questions will be scored. You will be able to refer to your answers as you write your essay in Part 2.

1 The word *impact* is used in the source "Handwritten Letters Are Important." What word has the same meaning as *impact*?

    a. effect

    b. letter

    c. emotion

    d. change

2 **Prose Constructed-Response** According to "Handwritten Letters Are Important," what is one advantage of writing a handwritten letter over writing an email?

_____

_____

_____

3 **Prose Constructed-Response** According to "Handwritten Letters Belong in the Past," how does technology keep electronic information from being lost?

_____

_____

_____

_____

Part 2 (85 minutes)

You now have 85 minutes to review your notes and sources and to plan, draft, revise, and edit your essay. While you may use your notes and refer to the sources, your essay must represent your original work. You may refer to your responses to the questions in Part 1, but you cannot change those answers. Now read your assignment and begin your work.

Your assignment

You have read two sources. Each text discusses handwritten letters. The two texts are:

- "Handwritten Letters Are Important"
- "Handwritten Letters Belong in the Past"

Consider the opinions on handwritten letters that are presented in the texts.

Write an essay that gives your opinion on whether people should send handwritten letters today. Remember to use reasons and evidence to support your opinion.

Now begin work on your essay. Manage your time carefully so that you can:

1. plan your essay

2. write your essay

3. revise and edit your final draft

Research Simulation

Informative Essay

Your Assignment

You will read two selections about Morse code. Then you will write an informative essay about the ways people have used Morse code to communicate.

Time Management: Informative Essay Task

Most formal writing tests are made up of two parts. Both parts of the tests are timed, so it's important to use your limited time wisely.

Part 1: Read Sources

35

35 minutes! That's not much time.

Preview the Assignment

→ 35 minutes

You will have 35 minutes to read two selections about Morse code. You will then answer questions about the sources.

Preview the questions. This will help you know which information you'll need to find as you read.

How Many?

How many pages of reading?

→ How many multiple-choice questions?

→ How many prose constructed-response questions?

Underline and take notes as you read. You probably won't have time to reread.

How do you plan to use the 35 minutes?

This is a lot to do in a short time.

Estimated time to read:

"__ __   ___ __   · __ ·   ··· ·
__ · __ ·   ___ ___   __ ·· ·"   [____] minutes

"The Many Uses of Morse Code"   [____] minutes

Estimated time to answer questions?   [____] minutes

Total   **35** minutes

Part 2: Write the Essay

Plan and Write an Informative Essay

85 minutes

You will have 85 minutes to plan, write, revise, and edit your essay.

How much time do you have? Pay attention to the clock!

Your Plan

Before you start to write, decide on a main idea for your essay and details that support your main idea.

How do you plan to use the 85 minutes?

Estimated time for planning the essay? ☐ minutes

Estimated time for writing? ☐ minutes

Be sure to leave enough time for this step!

Estimated time for editing? ☐ minutes

Estimated time for checking spelling, grammar, and punctuation? ☐ minutes

Total   85 minutes

Reread your essay, making sure that the points are clear. Check that there are no spelling or punctuation mistakes.

Your Assignment

> You will read two texts about Morse code. Then, you will write an informative essay about the ways people have used Morse code to communicate.

Complete the following steps as you plan and compose your essay.

1. Read an informational article about the invention of the telegraph and Morse code.

2. Read an informational article about different uses for Morse code.

3. Answer questions about the sources.

4. Plan, write, and revise your essay.

Part 1 (35 minutes)

You will now read the sources. Take notes on important facts and details as you read. You can refer to the sources and your notes as you write your essay.

-- ━- ━-━- ●-● ●●● ●

━●━ ● ━━━ ━●● ●

by Frank Hernandez

Before the mid-1800s, sending a message long-distance was no easy task. A letter or messenger could only travel as fast as a ship could sail or a horse could run. That could take days, weeks, or even months! Several American inventors set out to find a faster way to communicate over long distances using electricity. Among them was Samuel Morse. The group developed a way to send electrical impulses through wires.

10   However, only those impulses could be sent, and there was no way to understand what they might mean. So, Morse used the impulses to develop a code that came to be named after him. Morse code was made up of short signals, called dots, and long signals, called dashes. Originally, different combinations of dots and dashes stood for the numbers 0 through 9. This was later expanded to include the letters of the alphabet. Morse researched how often each letter appeared in English, and

20   gave the more common letters shorter codes. For example, the letters E and T are the most common, so they were written with just one signal.

By 1844, Morse was ready to demonstrate his invention to Congress. He sent a message through electrical wires from Baltimore to Washington D.C. Using Morse code, the modern telegraph was born.

A telegraph operator would tap out dots and dashes on a telegraph key, leaving spaces between letters and words. On the receiving end, the
30 impulses would cause a marker to write the dots and dashes on paper, and the operator would decode the message. Very soon, telegraph operators learned that they could understand messages just by listening. Skilled operators could send thirty words a minute.

Using Morse code through telegraph wires became very successful because it could be operated easily and didn't cost very much. It played a big part in the growth of the railroad, by allowing communication that improved scheduling
40 and reduced accidents. In turn, the railroad helped the telegraph spread even farther across the country. Dots and dashes played a key role in making the United States into what it is today!

The chart on the right shows how to determine the meaning of messages in Morse code (and the title of this text).

International Morse Code

1. A dash is equal to three dots
2. The space between parts of the same letter is equal to one dot.
3. The space between two letters is equal to three dots.
4. The space between two words is equal to seven dots.

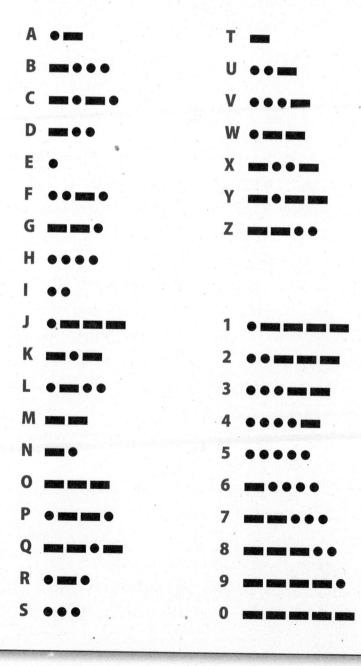

Notes

Am I on Track?

Actual Time Spent Reading

The Many Uses of Morse Code

by Peter Hoffman

On April 15, 1912, at 12:17 a.m., a distress call went out across the Atlantic Ocean.

SOS Titanic Position 41.44 N 50.24 W. Require immediate assistance. Come at once. We struck an iceberg. Sinking.

The message was sent out in Morse code by the Titanic. The "SOS" at the beginning of the message is a call for help. Those three letters are used because they are easy to remember and type in Morse code.
10 As you might know, the Titanic sank that night, and more than 1,500 people died. But thanks to Morse code messages sent between the Titanic and nearby ships, more than 700 people were saved from the icy waters of the Atlantic. Survivors also used Morse code to contact family and friends after their rescue and once they reached safety in New York.

Since its introduction in the 1840s, Morse code was used widely for over 160 years. It was the standard way ships communicated with each other,
20 especially in times of distress. Some ships sent wireless signals like the Titanic, while others flashed the dots and dashes using large lights.

Journalists used Morse code to deliver news around the world while it was still fresh. The code

also had many military uses. Ships and planes used it to pass information about enemy locations. Soldiers fighting on the front lines used wireless telegraphs to communicate with their commanders when the telephone lines were down or when the

30 connection was too poor to hear.

Morse code played an early part in the creation of another universal code. In 1948, Norman Woodland was trying to find a way to easily scan price information of products in supermarkets. He stretched the dots and dashes of Morse code downward to make bars, then made some of them wider and some narrower. While it would be several more decades before Woodland's code found its way into stores, it was the first version of what we now

40 know as the barcode.

Technology has provided many replacements for Morse code. By the end of the 1990s, ships stopped using it for distress signals. However, many amateur radio operators continue to keep Morse code alive. They learn it as a hobby and use it to communicate with other operators all across the world. A member of a Morse code club has even said that using Morse code, "you can sit back and hear a conversation. You aren't an operator until you hear the words."

Am I on Track?

Actual Time Spent Reading

© Houghton Mifflin Harcourt Publishing Company • Image Credits: © Houghton Mifflin Harcourt

Questions

Answer the following questions. You may refer to your reading notes. Your answers to these questions will be scored. You will be able to refer to your answers as you write your essay in Part 2.

1 The word *distress* is used in the source "The Many Uses of Morse Code." What word has the same meaning as *distress*?

  a. message

  b. symbol

  c. trouble

  d. relaxation

2 Which word or phrase best helps the reader understand the meaning of *distress*?

  a. "The "SOS" at the beginning of the message is a call for help."

  b. "... more than 700 people were saved from the icy waters of the Atlantic."

  c. "Survivors also used Morse code to send messages to family and friends after their rescue ..."

  d. "It was the standard way ships communicated with each other ..."

3 Which of the following claims could one make after reading these selections?

  a. Morse code did not have a major effect on the way people communicated.

  b. Morse code is no longer used today.

  c. Morse code is only used by ships.

  d. Morse code played a role in warfare.

4 Which detail best supports your answer to Question 3?

    a. "However, many amateur radio operators continue to keep Morse code alive."

    b. "The code also had many military uses."

    c. "Some ships sent wireless signals . . ."

    d. "Dots and dashes played a key role in making the United States into what it is today!"

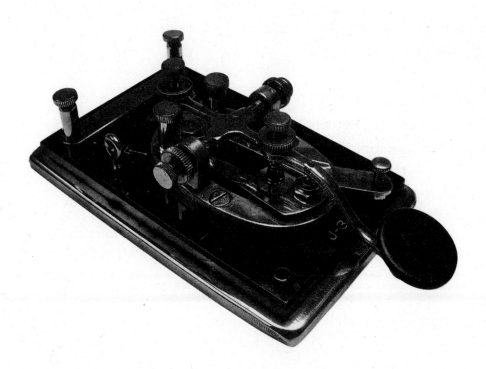

Part 2 (85 minutes)

You now have 85 minutes to review your notes and sources and to plan, draft, revise, and edit your essay. You may use your notes and refer to the sources, but your essay must represent your original work. You may refer to your responses to the questions in Part 1, but you cannot change those answers. Now read your assignment and begin your work.

Your assignment

You have read two sources about Morse code and how it has been used. The two texts are:

- "—— ——— •—• ••• •   —•—• ——— —•• •"
- "The Many Uses of Morse Code"

Think about the information on Morse code and its uses as it is presented in both texts.

Write an essay that explains the ways people have used Morse code to communicate. Remember to use textual evidence to develop your topic.

Now begin work on your essay. Manage your time carefully so that you can:

1. plan your essay

2. write your essay

3. revise and edit your final draft

Response to Literature

Your Assignment

You will read an excerpt from *Ben and Me.*
Then you will use what you have read to
write a response to literature explaining
how Amos's point of view affects his
description of Ben Franklin.

Time Management: Response to Literature Task

There are two parts to most formal writing tests. Both parts of the tests are timed, so it's important to use your limited time wisely.

Part 1: Read Sources

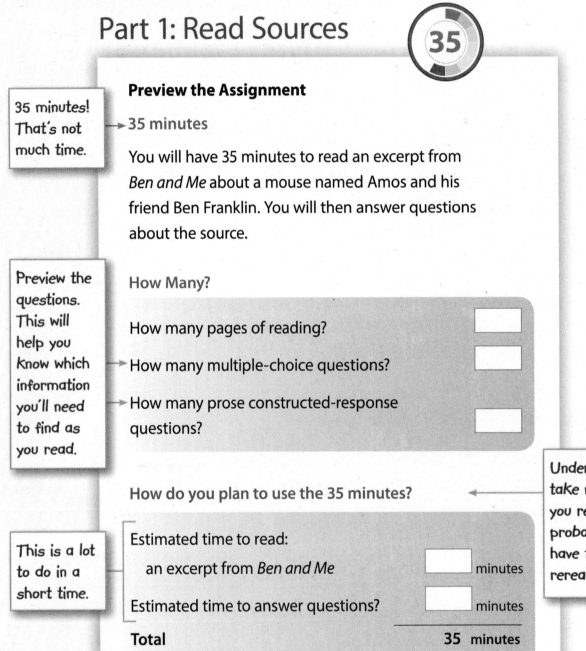

35

Preview the Assignment

→ 35 minutes

You will have 35 minutes to read an excerpt from *Ben and Me* about a mouse named Amos and his friend Ben Franklin. You will then answer questions about the source.

How Many?

How many pages of reading?

→ How many multiple-choice questions?

→ How many prose constructed-response questions?

How do you plan to use the 35 minutes?

Estimated time to read:

   an excerpt from *Ben and Me* [ ] minutes

Estimated time to answer questions? [ ] minutes

Total   **35 minutes**

35 minutes! That's not much time.

Preview the questions. This will help you know which information you'll need to find as you read.

This is a lot to do in a short time.

Underline and take notes as you read. You probably won't have time to reread.

Part 2: Write the Essay

Plan and Write a Response to Literature

85 minutes

You will have 85 minutes to plan, write, revise, and edit your response to literature.

Your Plan

Before you start to write, determine the main idea of your response to literature and the details that support your main idea.

How do you plan to use the 85 minutes?

Estimated time for planning the essay? ☐ minutes

Estimated time for writing? ☐ minutes

Estimated time for editing? ☐ minutes

Estimated time for checking spelling, grammar, and punctuation? ☐ minutes

Total   85 minutes

How much time do you have? Pay attention to the clock!

Be sure to leave enough time for this step!

Reread your essay, making sure that the points are clear. Check that there are no spelling or punctuation mistakes.

Your Assignment

> You will read a text and then write a response to literature that explains how Amos's point of view affects his description of Ben Franklin.

Complete the following steps as you plan and compose your response to literature.

1. Read an excerpt from *Ben and Me*.

2. Answer questions about the source.

3. Plan, write, and revise your response to literature.

Part 1 (35 minutes)

You will now read the source. Take notes on important details as you read. You can refer to the source and your notes as you write your essay.

Ben and Me

An Astonishing Life of Benjamin Franklin
By His Good Mouse Amos

By Robert Lawson

Since the recent death of my lamented friend and patron Ben Franklin, many so-called historians have attempted to write accounts of his life and his achievements. Most of these are wrong in so many respects that I feel the time has now come for me to take pen in paw and set things right.

All of these ill-informed scribblers seem astonished at Ben's great fund of information, at his brilliant decisions, at his seeming knowledge of all
10 that went on about him.

Had they asked me, I could have told them. It was ME.

For many years I was his closest friend and adviser and, if I do say it, was in great part responsible for his success and fame.

Not that I wish to claim too much: I simply hope to see justice done, credit given where credit is due, and that's to me—mostly.

Ben was undoubtedly a splendid fellow, a great
20 man, a patriot and all that; but he was undeniably stupid at times, and had it not been for me—well, here's the true story, and you can judge for yourself.

I was the oldest of twenty-six children. My parents, in naming us, went right through the alphabet. I, being first, was Amos, the others went along through Bathsheba, Claude, Daniel—and so forth down to the babies: Xenophon, Ysobel, and Zenas.

We lived in the vestry of Old Christ Church
30 on Second Street, in Philadelphia—behind the paneling. With that number of mouths to feed we were, naturally, not a very prosperous family. In fact we were really quite poor—as poor as church-mice.

But it was not until the Hard Winter of 1745 that things really became desperate. That was a winter long to be remembered for its severity, and night after night my poor father would come in tired and wet with his little sack practically empty.

We were driven to eating prayer-books, and
40 when those gave out we took to the Minister's sermons. That was, for me, the final straw. The prayer-books were tough, but those sermons!

Being the oldest, it seemed fitting that I should go out into the world and make my own way. Perhaps I could in some way help the others. At least, it left one less to be provided for.

So, saying farewell to all of them—my mother and father and all the children from Bathsheba to Zenas—I set forth on the coldest, windiest night of a
50 cold and windy winter.

Little did I dream, at that moment, of all the strange people and experiences I should encounter before ever I returned to that little vestry home!

All I thought of were my cold paws, my empty stomach—and those sermons. I have never known how far I traveled that night, for, what with the cold and hunger, I must have become slightly delirious. The first thing I remember clearly was being in a kitchen and smelling CHEESE! It didn't take long to find it; it was only a bit of rind and fairly dry, but how I ate!

Refreshed by this, my first real meal in many a day, I began to explore the house. It was painfully bare; clean, but bare. Very little furniture; and that all hard and shiny; no soft things, or dusty corners where a chap could curl up and have a good warm nap. It was cold too, almost as cold as outdoors.

Upstairs were two rooms. One was dark, and from it came the sound of snoring; the other had a light, and the sound of sneezing. I chose the sneezy one.

In a large chair close to the fireplace sat a short, thick, round-faced man, trying to write by the light of a candle. Every few moments he would sneeze, and his square-rimmed glasses would fly off. Reaching for these he would drop his pen; by the time he found that and got settled to write, the candle would flicker from the draught; when that

80 calmed down, the sneezing would start again, and so it went. He was not accomplishing much in the way of writing.

Of course I recognized him. Everyone in Philadelphia knew the great Doctor Benjamin Franklin, scientist, inventor, printer, editor, author, soldier, statesman and philosopher.

He didn't look great or famous that night, though, he just looked cold—and a bit silly.

He was wrapped in a sort of dressing-gown, with a dirty fur collar; and on his head was perched an 90 odd-looking fur cap.

The cap interested me, for I was still chilled to the bone—and this room was just as bleak as the rest of the house. It was a rather disreputable-looking affair, that cap; but in one side of it I had spied a hole—just about my size.

Up the back of the chair l went, and under cover of the next fit of sneezes, in I slid. What a cozy place that was! Plenty of room to move about a bit; just enough air; such soft fur, and such warmth!

100 "Here," said I to myself, "is my home. No more cold streets, or cellars, or vestries. HERE I stay."

At the moment, of course, I never realized how true this was to prove. All I realized was that I was warm, well fed and—oh, so sleepy!

And so to bed.

I slept late the next morning. When I woke my fur-cap home was hanging on the bedpost, and I in it.

Dr. Franklin was again crouched over the fire
110 attempting to write, between fits of sneezing and
glasses-hunting. The fire, what there was of it, was
smoking, and the room was as cold as ever.

"Not wishing to be critical—" I said. "But,
perhaps, a bit of wood on that smoky ember that you
seem to consider a fire might—"

"WASTE NOT, WANT NOT," said he, severe,
and went on writing.

"Well, just suppose," I said, "just suppose you
spend two or three weeks in bed with pewmonia—
120 that be a waste or—"

"It would be," said he, putting on a log; "whatever
your name might be."

"Amos," said I. . . . "And then there'd be doctors'
bills—"

"BILLS!" said he, shuddering, and put on two
more logs, quick. The fire blazed up then, and the
room became a little better, but not much.

"Dr. Franklin," I said, "that fireplace is all
wrong."

130 "You might call me Ben—just plain Ben," said
he. . . . "What's wrong with it?"

"Well, for one thing, most of the heat goes
up the chimney. And for another, you can't get
around it. Now, outside our church there used to
be a Hot-chestnut Man. Sometimes, when business
was rushing, he'd drop a chestnut. Pop was always
on the look-out, and almost before it touched the
ground he'd have it in his sack—and down to the

vestry with it. There he'd put it in the middle of the
140 floor—and we'd all gather round for the warmth.

"Twenty-eight of us it would heat, and the room
as well. It was all because it was OUT IN THE
OPEN, not stuck in a hole in the wall like that
fireplace."

"Amos," he interrupts, excited, "there's an idea
there! But we couldn't move the fire out into the
middle of the room."

"We could if there were something to put it in,
iron or something."

150 "But the smoke?" he objected.

"PIPE," said I, and curled up for another nap.

Am I on Track?

Actual Time Spent Reading

Questions

Answer the following questions. You may refer to your reading notes, and you should cite text evidence in your responses. Your answers to these questions will be scored. You will be able to refer to your answers as you write your essay in Part 2.

1 How does Amos describe the way other people see Ben Franklin?

   a. ill-informed and astonished

   b. lamented and a patron

   c. brilliant and knowledgeable

   d. stupid and a patriot

2 **Prose Constructed-Response** What is Amos and Ben's relationship, according to the beginning of this excerpt?

_____

_____

_____

_____

_____

3 **Prose Constructed-Response** How does Amos's life with his family affect his view of Ben's home?

_____

_____

_____

_____

Part 2 (85 minutes)

You now have 85 minutes to review your notes and the source and to plan, draft, revise, and edit your essay. While you may use your notes and refer to the source, your essay must represent your original work. You may refer to your responses to the questions in Part 1, but you cannot change those answers. Now read your assignment and begin your work.

Your assignment

You have read an excerpt from *Ben and Me*.

Write a response to literature that explains how Amos's point of view affects his description of Ben Franklin.

Now begin work on your essay. Manage your time carefully so that you can:

1. plan your essay

2. write your essay

3. revise and edit your final draft

Research Simulation

Narrative

Your Assignment

You will read two texts about electricity. Then you will write a narrative about living in a world where major sources of electricity have been shut down for over a year.

Time Management: Narrative Task

Most formal writing tests are made up of two parts. Both parts of the tests are timed, so it's important to use your limited time wisely.

Part 1: Read Sources

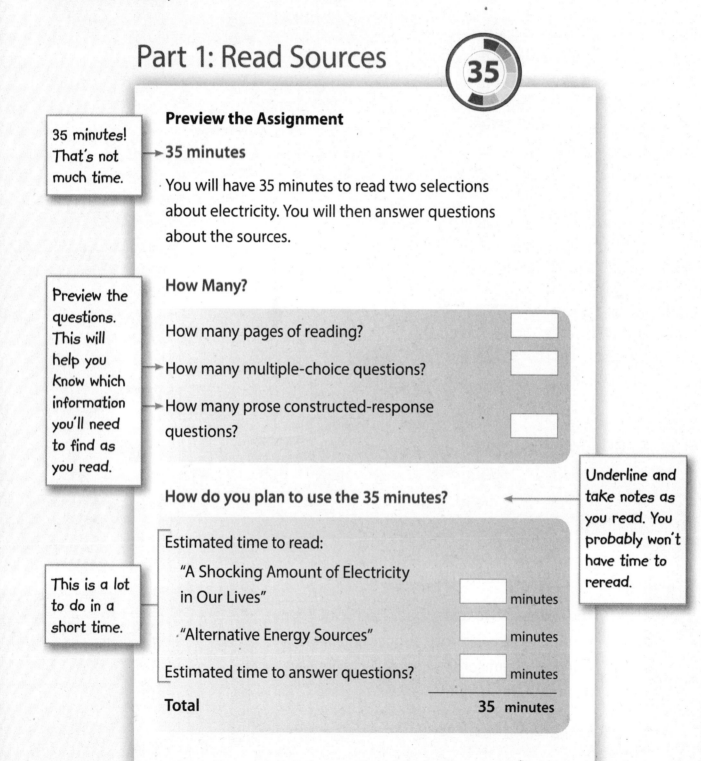

35

35 minutes! That's not much time.

Preview the Assignment

35 minutes

You will have 35 minutes to read two selections about electricity. You will then answer questions about the sources.

How Many?

Preview the questions. This will help you know which information you'll need to find as you read.

How many pages of reading?

How many multiple-choice questions?

How many prose constructed-response questions?

Underline and take notes as you read. You probably won't have time to reread.

How do you plan to use the 35 minutes?

This is a lot to do in a short time.

Estimated time to read:

"A Shocking Amount of Electricity in Our Lives" _____ minutes

"Alternative Energy Sources" _____ minutes

Estimated time to answer questions? _____ minutes

Total   **35** minutes

Part 2: Write the Narrative

Plan and Write a Narrative

85 minutes

You will have 85 minutes to plan, write, revise, and edit your story.

Your Plan

Before you start to write, determine the information from the sources you will use as a basis for your story. Then decide what will happen in your story.

How do you plan to use the 85 minutes?

Estimated time for planning the story? ☐ minutes

Estimated time for writing? ☐ minutes

Estimated time for editing? ☐ minutes

Estimated time for checking spelling, grammar, and punctuation? ☐ minutes

Total　　　　　　　　　　　　　 **85 minutes**

> How much time do you have? Pay attention to the clock!

> Be sure to leave enough time for this step!

> Reread your story, making sure that the points are clear. Check that there are no spelling or punctuation mistakes.

Your Assignment

You will read two texts. Then, you will write a narrative about life in a world where the electrical grid has been shut down for over a year.

Complete the following steps as you plan and compose your narrative.

1. Read a blog post about the uses of electricity in today's world.

2. Read a fact sheet about alternative sources of energy.

3. Answer questions about the sources.

4. Plan, write, and revise your story.

Part 1 (35 minutes)

You will now read the sources. Take notes on important facts and details as you read. You can refer to the sources and your notes as you write your story.

A Shocking Amount of Electricity in Our Lives

by Farrah Diaz

Whether you realize it or not, electricity is everywhere. You wouldn't be reading this blog post on the Internet without it. You couldn't watch TV, play video games, listen to the radio, or talk on the phone either. In fact, almost every part of our day is connected to electricity in one form or another.

Here are some examples. When you take a hot shower or bath, the reason the water is hot is because of an electric water heater. When you
10 cool your house with an air conditioner in the summer or heat it with a furnace in the winter, you use electricity, too (even gas furnaces use some electricity). Meals wouldn't be very tasty or good for you if you couldn't keep milk and vegetables in the refrigerator, or cook the food on a stove or in a microwave.

People who ride trains or subways also rely on electricity. But what if you drive a car? When you go to the gas station to fill up, electricity is what lets the
20 pumps actually move the gas into your car. In fact, most businesses use electricity in some way to make, sell, or move people and things.

Where does all this electricity come from? Most of the time it comes from the power grid. The grid is a system of wires that connects homes and businesses to the power plants that make electricity.

Blackouts, or times when the power goes out, happen when there are problems producing electricity at the plants or delivering it through
30 the wires. Blackouts remind us just how much we depend on electricity everyday, and how often we take it for granted.

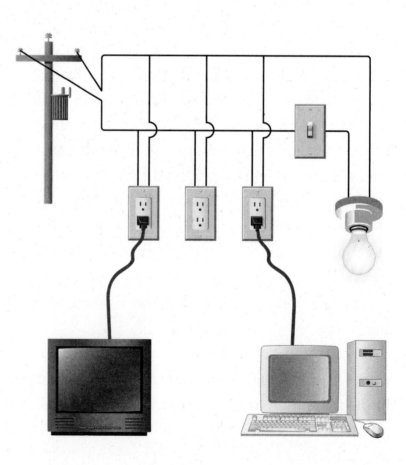

Alternative Energy Sources

About two-thirds of the electricity we use in the United States is produced using fossil fuels like coal, natural gas, and petroleum. These fuels are burned to make steam that powers a generator—a machine that changes energy to electricity. However, burning fuels creates a lot of pollution, so people have found alternative sources of energy.

Wind

Wind can turn blades on a device called a
10 turbine. The blades spin a shaft connected to a generator. Wind turbines can be small and used in homes, but many of them are taller than buildings. They are often grouped together in wind farms, creating a lot of power. Currently about 4 percent of electricity in the United States comes from wind.

Solar

Solar energy comes from the sun. It is captured by devices called solar cells that change the energy into electricity. Of course, electricity can be produced this way only when the sun in shining. However, batteries store the energy for use at night or when it's raining. Large solar cells can be placed on roofs to power houses. Small cells are even found in solar-powered calculators. Currently less than 1 percent of electricity in the United States comes from solar power.

Geothermal

Geothermal energy comes from heat deep within the earth. Hot, liquid rock called magma heats up underground water into steam. The steam is then used to power a generator to produce electricity. The water is then returned to the earth where it is heated up again. This lets energy be made with very little waste. Geothermal energy currently makes less than 1 percent of the electricity used in the United States.

Hydroelectric

Hydro means water, so hydroelectric power is electricity produced by moving water. Here's how it works: Water is held by a dam in a reservoir above a power plant. Water is then allowed to run into the power plant, where it powers a generator. A hydroelectric power plant you might have heard of is the Hoover Dam, on the border of Arizona and Nevada. It provides power to several states. Hydroelectric power makes up about 7 percent of the electricity used in the United States.

Am I on Track?

Actual Time Spent Reading

Questions

Answer the following questions. You may refer to your reading notes, and you should cite text evidence in your responses. Your answers to these questions will be scored. You will be able to refer to your answers as you write your story in Part 2.

1 How does a geothermal power plant produce electricity?

   a. It burns coal to heat water into steam.

   b. It changes the sun's energy into electricity.

   c. It uses magma to heat water into steam.

   d. It uses wind to power a generator.

2 **Prose Constructed-Response** Think about the uses of electricity in "A Shocking Amount of Electricity in Our Lives." What is the biggest problem you would face if the power went out?

_____

_____

_____

_____

3 **Prose Constructed-Response** How might solar power be helpful in a situation where the power grid stopped working? Cite text evidence in your response.

_____

_____

_____

_____

© Houghton Mifflin Harcourt Publishing Company

Part 2 (85 minutes)

You now have 85 minutes to review your notes and the source and to plan, draft, revise, and edit your narrative. While you may use your notes and refer to the source, your story must represent your original work. You may refer to your responses to the questions in Part 1, but you cannot change those answers. Now read your assignment and begin your work.

Your assignment

You have read two sources about electricity. The two texts are:

- "A Shocking Amount of Electricity in Our Lives"
- "Alternative Energy Sources"

Write a narrative about life in a world where the electrical grid has been shut down for over a year.

Now begin work on your narrative. Manage your time carefully so that you can:

1. plan your story

2. write your story

3. revise and edit your final draft

Excerpt from *Ben and Me: A New and Astonishing Life of Benjamin Franklin as Written by His Good Mouse Amos* by Robert Lawson. Copyright 1939 by Robert Lawson. Copyright renewed © 1967 by John W. Boyd. Reprinted by permission of The Permissions Company on behalf of Hachette Book Group, Inc.

Fly Away Home by Eve Bunting. Text copyright © 1991 by Eve Bunting. Illustrations copyright © 1991 by Ronald Himler. Reprinted by permission of Houghton Mifflin Harcourt Publishing Company.